MODERN LEGAL THEORY AND JUDICIAL IMPARTIALITY

Ofer Raban

BA (City College of New York), JD (Harvard), D Phil (Oxford)

London • Sydney • Portland, Oregon

First published in Great Britain 2003 by
The GlassHouse Press, The Glass House,
Wharton Street, London WC1X 9PX, United Kingdom
Telephone: + 44 (0)20 7278 8000   Facsimile: + 44 (0)20 7278 8080
Email: info@cavendishpublishing.com
Website: www.cavendishpublishing.com

Published in the United States by The GlassHouse Press, Cavendish Publishing,
c/o International Specialized Book Services,
5824 NE Hassalo Street, Portland,
Oregon 97213-3644, USA

Published in Australia by The GlassHouse Press,
45 Beach Street, Coogee, NSW 2034, Australia
Telephone: + 61 (2)9664 0909   Facsimile: + 61 (2)9664 5420
Email: info@cavendishpublishing.com.au
Website: www.cavendishpublishing.com.au

© Ofer Raban 2003

The GlassHouse Press is an imprint of Cavendish Publishing Limited

British Library Cataloguing in Publication Data
Raban, Ofer
Modern legal theory & judicial impartiality
1 Law – Philosophy 2 Jurisprudence 3 Judicial ethics 4 Justice
I Title
340.1'1

Library of Congress Cataloguing in Publication Data
Data available

ISBN 1-904385-07-9

1 3 5 7 9 10 8 6 4 2

Printed and bound in Great Britain by MPG Books Ltd, Bodmin, Cornwall

Acknowledgments

I would like to thank Beverley Brown, Jamie Hyatt, Mati Rabban and Nicos Stavropoulos for their very helpful comments.

Foreword

This book looks at various legal theories with the following perspective in mind: it examines their view on the *impartiality of legal interpretation*. As I hope to show, this perspective holds an important key to the understanding of many jurisprudential claims and disputes. The book, which deals with a number of schools of thought, is structured around two principal (and rival) theorists – HLA Hart and Ronald Dworkin. What is the justification for the emphasis on these two scholars? The short answer is that the Hart/Dworkin debate contains the principal difficulties with which legal theory has been recently occupying itself. But the full answer has something to do with the position of Hart's and Dworkin's theories in relation to other jurisprudential writings. Legal theories (and social theories in general) can be seen as stretching along a continuum beginning with claims that are true but trivial (for example, the claim that 'some legal questions have clear answers'[1]) and ending with claims that are astounding but wrong (for example, the claim that 'there is one right answer to any legal question'). Unsurprisingly, most scholarship occupies the middle ground between these extremes: it roams the somewhat uneventful territory of the qualified and sensible hypothesis. Such scholarship is not totally trivial, and it may very well be true, but it usually holds little hope for any significant insights. Both novices and experts may have more to gain from an in-depth analysis of the extreme – even if erroneous – positions: these strong claims may be wrong, but they may bring into sharp focus a potentially important perspective on the discipline. Nonetheless, one must exercise extreme caution here: it is difficult to mount an insightful defence of an ultimately erroneous position. This is where the emphasis on HLA Hart and Ronald Dworkin finds its justification: both Hart and Dworkin defend extreme and erroneous positions in a highly edifying manner. Moreover, both Hart and Dworkin defend positions that are *constructive* rather than *critical*: their theories are paradigms of the search for an impartial legal interpretation. As such, they often constitute a necessary background to many critical theories –

---

1   This is obviously a caricature, yet the chief propositions of some jurisprudential writings are not very far off. Here are two distinguished examples: 'If arguments for radical indeterminacy are valid, they may raise serious doubts about the possibility of legitimate, nonarbitrary legal systems and adjudicative procedures. In this Article, I defend the claim that the indeterminacy of the law is no more than moderate and reject critical legal scholars' arguments for radical indeterminacy.' Kress, 1989, p 283. 'The nihilism I have addressed is based on the premise that for any [legal] text there are any number of possible meanings and the interpreter creates a meaning by choosing one. I have accepted this premise, but have tried to deny the nihilism by showing why the freedom is not absolute.' Fiss, 1982, p 762.

some equally extreme and insightful – whose most basic project, as we shall see, is to deny such impartiality. Ultimately, however, this book goes beyond an analysis of the available literature: its last chapters are an attempt at a fresh and original contribution, focusing on the formal constraints of proper legal interpretation.

Contents

Chapter 1
Introduction: law and impartiality

We all agree that judges must apply the law *impartially*. What do we mean by that? According to the dictionary, impartiality pertains to 'equal treatment': partiality is a bias, a slant, a bent; impartiality does not tend towards either side. These spatial metaphors are of limited value: a judge is to treat both sides equally – but in what way? Surely the *resolution* can hardly treat equally both sides. But then impartiality resides not in the resolution but in the *decision-making process*: we need to know the *reasons* leading to a resolution in order to assess whether partiality is an appropriate charge. A partial resolution is reached through a reasoning process that is skewed in some way. But then again, in what way?

To be partial towards something is to have a *preference* for it. Partial adjudication consists in giving preference to a certain person, or a certain group, or a certain interest, or a certain ideology, or even a certain moral position. Now obviously, a judge may prefer a person or a group or an ideology *without* being partial: a preference for an honest litigant over a dishonest one, or a preference for a democratic form of government, would not constitute condemnable judicial partiality. The sort of preferences which implicate the danger of partiality must be, in some way, *unjustifiable*.

Preferences can be unjustifiable because they are wrong; or they can be unjustifiable because they appear to be neither right *nor* wrong (hence 'unjustifiable'): we say of some beliefs that they are 'simply a matter of preference', suggesting that they are not open to a contradictory demonstration. These preferences are controversial: to call something a 'preference' is to point to the fact that others do not prefer it. It is this latter group of unjustifiable preferences which causes the gravest concern to legal theorists, because the danger of these preferences playing a role in adjudication (of judges making legal determinations being swayed by such preferences) is enormous. Many of our respectable political, moral, and social beliefs appear to belong to this category of preferences; and, unsurprisingly, these are tremendously relevant to the resolution of countless legal disputes. Beliefs concerning the obligations that people owe each other, the appropriate limits of governmental powers, the sort of guarantees that society owes its individual members, and many more – all appear to include numerous matters of preference (and all are highly pertinent to countless legal questions and disputes). And yet, their use may constitute partiality. What's more, we tend to think that these preferences often reflect the *self-interest* of the beholder: many think, for example, that opinions on the importance of material equality are a matter of preference, and nobody is surprised that poor people tend to consider material equality as far more important than rich people do. Thus, if judges employ such preferences in their decision-making process, legal determinations may be skewed in the most ominous of ways – through the self-interest of the decision-makers (including, for example, the self-interest of their social or economic or ethnic class).

This difficulty is a major preoccupation of modern legal theory. The central project of many theories is to establish the impartiality of proper legal interpretation (by describing a methodology which excludes preferences from that decision-making process) – while many of their opponents seek to debunk that impartiality.[1] Few discussions in legal theory actually employ the concept of impartiality; but that concept looms large over many claims and disputes, lending them much of their significance. So approaching the study of jurisprudence with the (rather straightforward) issue of impartiality in mind affords a superb perspective on today's central jurisprudential debates. Who is *correct* in these disputes is to be judged, of course, by the merits of the respective arguments, and this book will examine these arguments closely – often engaging in rather detailed analysis. But the book will consistently return to impartiality as a platform from which to survey the meaning and significance of these controversies.

Our look at legal theories, and their relation to the notion of impartiality, begins with modern legal positivism and the theory of HLA Hart – thereby skipping all of Hart's positivist predecessors. The reason for this is simple: Hart's theory is a clear and straightforward formulation of legal positivism, and a conscious attempt to overcome some of the shortcomings of previous positivist theorising. The book also ignores the theory of natural law, which dominated the scene for many years, and which was demolished and replaced by the rise of legal positivism. The reason for this is that the problem with which we are concerned – that of judicial impartiality – takes a radical turn in the modern age with the expanding notion of preferences. According to natural law theory, legal interpretation must be guided by universal moral truths, which are, in principle, accessible to man. It is only when preferences came to encompass *moral* beliefs – as they so spectacularly did in the modern age – that natural law theory came to be regarded as unacceptable. Indeed, it is only when moral choices became 'relativised' that the problem of judicial impartiality assumed the prominence which, under various titles, it still enjoys today. Natural law theory truly belongs to a different age: its demise coincided with the demise of the old moral, religious, and metaphysical grounding which also brought the problem of judicial impartiality to the fore. This is not to say, of course, that natural law theory does not concern itself with impartiality; it certainly does! Impartiality is a concern for any theory of legal regulation. It is just that the solution of natural law to that problem –

---

1 Joseph Singer puts a somewhat similar point in the following way: 'many current scholars ... attempt to recreate, to some extent, the idea of an objective standpoint that judges can use to adjudicate complex legal issues without taking sides in desperate social struggles. Each of these schools attempts to answer the question "why isn't that just your opinion?" by reference either to an impartial criterion for judgment ... or a neutral decision procedure for adjudicating claims ...' Singer, 1988, pp 516–17.

grounding proper adjudication in universally valid principles of human morality – is no longer a serious option for us today. Nevertheless, legal positivism came to dominate legal theory not merely by spurning the solution offered by natural law, but by offering its own solution to that problem. It is to that solution, and to the legal positivism of HLA Hart, that we now turn.

Chapter 2
The legal positivism of HLA Hart

I Hart's thesis

The theories of law with which this book is concerned attempt to explain what makes a legal claim or a legal proposition *legally valid*: they offer a description of how it is determined that the law requires X, or that it does not require Y. Those theories that aim at establishing the *impartiality* of legal determinations seek to exclude the use of *preferences* from that decision-making process: establishing what the law requires, they say, is a decision-making process which doesn't take preferences into account. HLA Hart's theory of law is such a theory. It is also a theory that is surprisingly commonsensical. According to Hart, the law is a collection of rules whose status as *legal* rules is a consequence of some official action (they are, for the most part, declared by a legislature or by courts); and the application of these legal rules involves a determination of whether a case falls *inside* or *outside* the conventional meaning of the words appearing in them. Section I of this chapter will elaborate and explain these claims, and will also examine how they seek to solve the problem of judicial impartiality. Sections II and III will criticise Hart's claims, as well as his solution to the impartiality problem. Section IV will briefly survey the state of legal positivism after Hart.

Identifying the authoritative legal rules

Hart's theory of law, appearing in its most complete formulation in *The Concept of Law*, articulates roughly two stages for determining what the law requires (two stages of legal interpretation): the first involves the identification of legal rules, the second the identification of the requirements of these rules vis-à-vis a particular case.[1] Together these two processes establish what the law says – or whether it says anything – on any given matter.

According to Hart, all mature legal systems have a test for the identification of legal rules, a test which all legal practitioners know and agree upon. Hart calls this test the 'rule of recognition'. Only rules which satisfy that test are recognised as *legal* rules (rather than moral rules, or social rules, or what have you).[2] The 'rule of recognition' specifies certain 'sources of law' where legal rules are to be found: these sources include the collection of statutes passed by parliament, judicial precedents, the decisions of administrative agencies, and other such authorities.[3] If a rule is found in those specified sources, it is a legal

---

1 Hart, 1994.

2 Hart, 1994, p 116.

3 Hart says that 'the criteria for identifying the law are multiple and commonly include a written constitution, enactment by legislature, and judicial decisions'. Hart, 1994, p 101.

rule; if it ain't there – it ain't legal. As there are various legal sources in a complex, modern legal system, these sources are ranked for *relative supremacy* within the 'rule of recognition' (for example, the 'rule of recognition' may declare that a legislated statute is superior to a judicial precedent): this guarantees that it will be possible to identify one authoritative legal rule in cases where rules taken from different sources conflict. The 'rule of recognition' is, therefore, a rather complex theoretical entity: it contains references to various legal sources, as well as a ranking of these legal sources in order of supremacy. It may take quite a few pages to put this 'rule of recognition' on paper. Yet, however complex or lengthy, the 'rule of recognition' must be *shared* by the legal practitioners of the legal system to which it belongs: they must *agree* as to what is the governing 'rule of recognition'. The legal practitioners must share the test for the identification of legal rules.

According to Hart, it is the very fact that practitioners share the 'rule of recognition' that *constitutes* that rule: the 'rule of recognition', says Hart, *exists* by virtue of being accepted as a normative standard and followed. What does Hart mean by that? He means that the 'rule of recognition' exists as the test for valid legal rules because people accept it as a test and abide by it: it is, in other words, a *conventional* standard. Here is an analogy: the meaning of a word is what it is by virtue of its being accepted as such – that is, by virtue of the fact that we all agree that this is its meaning. The meaning of a word is also a *conventional* standard; it is constituted by conventional agreement. (Indeed it has been suggested that Hart's idea that the 'rule of recognition' is a conventional standard has linguistic conventions as its very model.[4]) Thus, just as the correct meaning of words (or the correct test for using them) is supposedly constituted by conventional agreement among speakers, so is the 'rule of recognition' (or the correct test for the legal validity of rules) constituted by agreement among those who are practising law.

Now Hart concedes that the 'rule of recognition' is not explicitly articulated, and certainly not in its entirety: people are not in the habit of citing a 'rule of recognition' when they identify legal rules.[5] Nevertheless, says Hart, we know the rule exists, and we know what it requires, because this is '*shown* in the way in which particular rules are identified, either by courts or other officials or private persons or their advisors'.[6] One can detect the 'rule of recognition' by observing the way in which people (private individuals, lawyers, judges, state officials) identify legal rules: people look for legal rules in certain 'sources of law' (the pronouncements of the legislator, the decisions of courts, the promulgations of administrative agencies), and in doing so they follow the 'rule of recognition' – thereby making it known. What's more, deducing the 'rule of recognition' from the actions of these people does not involve any complicated evaluative or controversial reasoning: according to Hart, this is a

---

4   Stavropoulos, 2001.

5   Hart, 1994, p 101.

6   Hart, 1994, p 101 (original emphasis).

straightforward factual observation as to where people go when they look for legal rules.[7]

So the 'rule of recognition' – which can be identified by observing the actions of legal practitioners – points practitioners to the 'sources of law' where legal rules can be found. Sometimes the source will not present the practitioner with a 'ready-to-use' rule: Hart thinks that judicial decisions, for example, may lay down a precedent without explicitly articulating its governing rule.[8] In such cases, the person seeking the legal rule must *extract* the rule from the precedent before her (she must grasp the rule laid down by the precedent). Yet, ultimately, all rules of law are linguistically formulated rules using general classifications: Hart says that 'all rules involve recognising or classifying particular cases as instances of general terms'; rules of law 'refer to *classes* of persons, and to *classes* of acts, thing, circumstance; and [the law's] successful operation … depends on a widely diffused capacity to recognise particular acts, things, and circumstances as instances of the general classification which the law makes'.[9] In short, the law consists of rules, found in certain recognised sources identified by the 'rule of recognition'; and these rules divide the world into classes of 'acts, things, or circumstances' using general words (for instance, the class of 'assaults', the class of 'contractual agreements', or the class of being 'unemployed'), and then prescribe the treatment that is to be accorded each of these classes.

Applying legal rules

Once the legal rule is identified, establishing what the law requires on any given case is a rather straightforward exercise in linguistic classification: according to Hart, the legal interpreter applies the law by examining whether the case (or the hypothetical instance) falls inside or outside the conventional meaning of the classificatory term of the relevant legal rule. For example, if a rule reads 'no vehicles in the park', then whether the rule is or is not violated by a certain conduct depends on whether that conduct involves a 'vehicle' and a 'park' according to the conventional meanings of these terms.

Now general terms have cases of clear and certain applications – 'General terms would be useless to us as a medium of communication unless there were such familiar, generally unchallenged cases'[10] – as well as cases of uncertain applications: take any general term, says Hart, and you will find that it has some applications regarding which it is unclear whether it applies or not. The term 'silk', for example, has unmistakable applicability to a certain substance

---

7   Indeed it is difficult to imagine how the 'rule of recognition' could be shared if potentially controversial evaluations were required for its very identification.

8   According to Hart judicial precedents are sources of law which do not contain explicit rules but instead indicate the rules 'by ostentation' (note again the similarities with language, which is often learned by ostentation).

9   Hart, 1994, pp 123–24 (original emphasis).

10 Hart, 1994, p 126.

secreted by silkworms; but imagine that we discover that the substance somewhat changes its chemical constitution when exposed to certain pollutants. This would present us with an uncertain case of applicability: the altered material is a borderline case falling in the 'penumbra', or the 'open texture', of the term 'silk'. ('Open-textured' and 'penumbral' were the adjectives Hart used to denote uncertain cases of application.[11]) What, for Hart, distinguishes core applications from borderline applications? Core applications are those characterised by *agreement*: the 'plain case' is one where 'there is general agreement in judgment as to the applicability of the classifying term' – whereas a borderline case of applicability occurs where 'no firm convention or general agreement dictates its use'.[12] In this latter case, the determination of applicability is not resolved by the meaning of the general term: the question whether the altered material is 'silk' or not 'silk' cannot be answered by consulting the *meaning* of that term, because meaning is presumably a function of convention, and there is no convention governing the matter. We may summon various arguments in deciding whether the altered material falls inside or outside the term 'silk' – and some arguments would be better, some worse; but no position would be 'correct' or 'incorrect' as far as the *meaning* of our term is concerned. Hart says that 'if in such cases doubts are to be resolved, something in the nature of a choice between open alternatives must be made by whoever is to resolve them'.[13] ('Open alternatives' here signifies that neither option is uniquely correct.) So once we encounter a borderline case, we must make a choice regarding the applicability of the term: the meaning of the term does not settle the issue. But in 'core' cases there is no such choice: applicability is determined by linguistic conventions which leave no room for any 'open alternatives'.

This means, for Hart, that *legal rules* follow a similar pattern – since their applicability is a function of the applicability of the general terms appearing in them. Hart says that 'in case of everything which we are prepared to call a rule, it is possible to distinguish clear central cases, where it certainly applies, and others where there are reasons for both asserting and denying that it applies. Nothing can eliminate this duality of a core of certainty and a penumbra of doubt when we are engaged in bringing particular situations under general rules'.[14] There are core cases for the application of legal rules – for example, those involving core instances of 'vehicles' and 'parks'; and there are cases where the rule's application is unclear – for example, when it is unclear

---

11 That uncertainty, for Hart, was an ever-present possibility. He said that 'Uncertainty at the borderline is the price to be paid for the use of general classifying terms in any form of communication concerning matters of fact. Natural languages like English are when so used irreducibly open-textured'. Hart, 1994, p 128.

12 Hart, 1994, pp 126–27.

13 Hart, 1994, p 127. The arguments for and against the applicability of a borderline case are arguments about 'whether the present case resembles the plain case "sufficiently" in "relevant" respects'. This, for Hart, is a question whose answer lacks a truth value – it is neither true nor false.

14 Hart, 1994, p 123.

whether the relevant object is a 'vehicle' (say, the object is a motorised wheelchair). When such cases occur in the application of legal rules, we shall have to go beyond what the law says: we shall have to appeal to considerations external to the law in deciding the applicability of the rule, and no answer will be correct or incorrect as far as the law or existing legal requirements are concerned.

It is, of course, an uninteresting truism that there are cases where the law is clear ('core' cases) and cases where it is unclear ('penumbral' cases); but Hart is offering an *explanation* of what makes legal cases clear or unclear. According to Hart, the core and penumbra of the law track the core and penumbra of the general classificatory terms appearing in legal rules. In other words, whether a case is a clear case for the law is a function of whether it is a clear case of applicability for the general terms appearing in the relevant legal rule.[15] Where the applicability of the general terms is uncertain, the law is uncertain. Indeed when judges decide the applicability of a rule in a borderline case they 'have settled a question as to the meaning, for the purposes of this rule, of a general word'.[16]

So legal rules have core cases of applicability when a case is a core case for the application of their general terms; and they have borderline cases of applicability when a case is a borderline case for the applicability of their general terms. Since what the law requires is simply a function of what the conventional meanings of the general classificatory terms require, when the applicability of these terms is unclear, the legal interpreter must go 'outside the law' in order to determine the applicability of the relevant legal rule. In such cases the law has no clear answer on the matter, and it is no help to keep staring at the law. If there is a decision to be made, the legal interpreter will have to go somewhere else in order to make it. At this point, if the case is in court, the judge must move from the task of legal interpretation (from establishing what the law is) to the task of judicial legislation (to establishing what the law *should* be): from the task of identifying the law to the task of writing it.

Nevertheless, according to Hart such cases are a minority existing only on the 'margins of rules':[17] given the *communicative* function of linguistic terms, the questionable cases – those regarding which it is indeterminate whether they fall within or without a term – are few. Hart says that 'failure to do justice to [the phenomenon of open texture] will always provoke exaggeration';[18] in

---

15 Hart says that there are cases where 'there are reasons both for and against the use of a general term, and no firm convention or general agreement dictates its use … At this point the authoritative general language in which the rule is expressed may guide only in an uncertain way much as an authoritative example does … [S]ubsumption and the drawing of a syllogistic conclusion no longer characterize the nerve of reasoning involved in determining what is the right thing to do'. Hart, 1994, pp 126–27.

16 Hart, 1994, p 129.

17 Hart, 1994, p 135.

18 Hart, 1994, p 136.

reality 'the life of the law consists to a very large extent in the guidance both of officials and private individuals by determinate rules which … do not require from them a fresh judgment from case to case'.[19] Just as our everyday use of language encounters few questionable borderline cases, so does the law – whose applicability is a function of the applicability of our natural language – mostly handle clear and unambiguous cases.

Hart's theory and impartiality

It is easy to see how Hart's theory establishes the impartiality of proper legal interpretation. To begin with, legal rules are identified by the 'rule of recognition', and everybody agrees what that rule is: it is a conventional standard. People identify legal rules by following the same procedure that everybody else follows. Identifying legal rules is therefore a decision-making process having no place for considerations of preference. Preferences are by definition controversial; conventions are by definition a matter of consensus. If identifying legal rules is a matter of following a conventionally accepted standard, then there is no danger of partiality in the process of identifying legal rules. Moreover, in most cases there is no danger of partiality in the *application* of these rules either: their applications are, too, grounded in conventions – in linguistic conventions regarding the correct use of general terms. Whether a case falls within or without a general classificatory term is, for the most part, a determination with no place for considerations of preference.

Admittedly, there are cases where no convention governs the applicability or inapplicability of a general term (no convention on the use of the term 'vehicle' establishes whether a motorised wheelchair is or is not a 'vehicle'). When such instances occur, no convention establishes the correct legal determination, and the legal interpreter must resort to arguments about the pros and cons of finding the term, and thereby the rule, applicable. Here, partiality may rear its head: preferences may certainly influence some of these determinations. Yet, as we saw, these cases are a small minority – they are the exception, rather than the rule.[20] Moreover, these are not cases of ascertaining what the law requires; these are cases of ascertaining what the law *should* require – meaning that preferences may be used only in cases where the law does not resolve the issue in question. There are gaps in the law. Cases may arise that nobody has contemplated; the legislature may do a bad job or neglect its duties, or may even intentionally leave some areas unregulated: in such cases legal interpreters must go beyond the law. But what else can they do? Legal cases must be resolved, and refusing to hear a case merely amounts to handing the victory to defendants. Nevertheless, to repeat, *legal interpretation* (establishing what the law says – not what it should say) is an activity that is *necessarily* impartial; and the majority of cases involve legal

---

19 Hart, 1994, p 135.
20 See Hart, 1994, pp 131–32.

interpretation. Determining legal rights and duties is, for the most part, a straightforward business revolving around the use of readily available conventional standards, so that in the majority of cases partiality is not even a possibility for the conscientious legal interpreter.

II   Hart and the problem of 'essentially contested concepts'

There are two principal problems with Hart's picture of legal interpretation. The first concerns what have come to be known as 'essentially contested concepts'. (My discussion will use the words 'term' and 'concept' interchangeably.) Many linguistic terms do not sit well with Hart's analysis of the core and the penumbra: they do not have large cores of certain applications upon which everybody agrees. Instead, their applications are very commonly disputed, and, as far as the speaker is concerned, correct applicability may have little to do with whether everybody else does or does not agree. This brings into question the sense in which the application of rules is a function of conventional agreement, and it threatens to sap much explanatory power out of Hart's theory. The second problem, which I will address in section III, concerns a different but more fundamental difficulty: viz, practitioners' habitual disregard for the 'boundaries' set by the linguistic meaning of the terms appearing in legal rules.

On essentially contested concepts and their containment

Hart's understanding of linguistic terms having large cores of conventional agreement and marginal penumbras of disagreement does not sit well with a whole range of rather common terms.[21] They have been named, among other things, 'essentially contested concepts' – concepts like 'justice', 'democracy', 'art', or 'good faith', regarding which speakers have different, and often competing, understandings.[22] Essentially contested concepts do have applications upon which everybody agrees, but these applications are not as common: where essentially contested concepts are concerned, there is no good reason to think – as Hart does – that the penumbral cases (those cases where people disagree about applications) are a marginal minority. It would appear, instead, that each time a contested concept or expression is involved,

---

21 Some scholars believe that Hart's understanding is not applicable to *any* term. According to Nicos Stavropoulos, there is little justification for the distinction Hart draws between core and penumbral applications, because conventional agreement may be proven wrong. According to Stavropoulos, there is no important difference between decisions of applicability in so-called borderline cases and decisions of applicability in the core – both are responsible to arguments and justifications of applicability: both, that is, are responsible to theory. Stavropoulos, 1996.

22 This notion was introduced in a famous 1956 article by William Gallie. See Gallie, 1956. The notion has had an important role to play in legal theory, as it was picked up by Ronald Dworkin and developed into his famous concept/conception distinction. See Dworkin, 1977, p 103. Dworkin credits John Rawls with the distinction. See Rawls, 1971, p 5. Rawls, funnily enough, attributes the distinction to Hart. See Hart, 1994, pp 155–59.

disagreement is the rule rather than the exception. Moreover, essentially contested concepts (such as 'reasonableness', 'recklessness', 'excessive force', 'unfair dealing', 'coercion', and 'excessive burden') figure as classificatory general terms in innumerable legal rules, and those exceptional cases that *do* generate consensus are not likely to arise in the judicial context. In short, Hart's claim that the 'life of the law' consists of clear and unambiguous cases, and that 'judicial legislation' is the exception rather than the rule, is simply wrong as far as essentially contested concepts are concerned; and there are an awful lot of essentially contested concepts in the law.[23]

Hart is not oblivious to this obvious point; he explicitly acknowledges the problem when discussing what he calls 'very general' classificatory terms whose applicability is *usually* controversial: 'Of course, even with very general standards there will be plain indisputable examples of what does, or does not, satisfy them. Some extreme cases of what is, or is not, a "fair rate" ... will always be identifiable *ab initio* ... But these are only the extremes of a range of different factors and are not likely to be met in practice.'[24] This, says Hart, 'entails a relative indeterminacy ... and a need for further official choice'.[25] However, Hart thinks that this is not a serious problem for his theory, because he thinks that such legal standards are *purged* – rendered determinate – by subsequent court decisions (the further 'official choice' he mentions): where a standard like 'reasonableness' appears in a legal rule, individuals 'are required to conform to a variable standard *before* it has been officially defined, and they may learn from a court only *ex post facto* when they have violated what, in terms of specific actions or forbearances, is the standard required of them. Where the decisions of the court on such matters are regarded as precedents, this specification of the variable standard is very like the exercise of delegated rule-making power by an administrative body ...'.[26] In other words, such legal standards are a mere delegation of authority for the courts to lay down the *real* legal rule containing the *real* legal standard.

---

23 It is worth noting that Ronald Dworkin has objected to Hart on the grounds that the concept of 'law' is *itself* an essentially contested concept. See Dworkin, 1986, pp 45–46. (Dworkin has changed his terminology several times in earlier and in subsequent writings, settling in *Law's Empire* on the notion of an 'interpretative concept'; yet what underlies that notion is no different from what underlies the notion of 'essentially contested concepts'.) Dworkin concludes from this that legal practice, and the task of identifying legal rights and duties, are not a matter of following conventional criteria. Dworkin also thinks that Hart's theory is a result of believing (erroneously – as essentially contested concepts seem to demonstrate) that the correct application of concepts is always a function of conventional criteria. There has been much criticism of Dworkin's claims, and a rather academic debate has developed around the essential contestedness of the concept of 'law'. See Hart, 1994, pp 246–47; Endicott, 1998, p 288.

24 Hart, 1994, pp 131–32.

25 Hart, 1994, pp 131–32.

26 Hart, 1994, p 132.

Putting aside the question of systems where court decisions are *not* regarded as precedents, Hart's claim remains highly questionable. One way of reading his argument is that courts *replace* vague and indeterminate standards (or 'essentially contested' terms) with other more determinate ones – that is, with standards with substantial cores of conventional agreement. Although there can be little doubt that courts applying standards like 'reasonableness', 'due care' or 'unfair competition' give these more determinate contents – indeed this they must do if only by recounting the facts of the case – it is doubtful that courts *replace* those standards, at least to the extent that they shun the use of equally vague and indeterminate terms. Courts habitually go back to the vague formulations, even if in each individual case they strive to give them a more precise articulation. The concept of 'negligence', for example, has received a large variety of formulations at the hands of courts; but only those formulations using equally vague concepts (for example, those defining negligence as 'a failure to exercise the due care expected of a reasonable person') approach the status of 'replacement' for this extremely contested term. In fact, Hart's idea that these formulations just wait to be given permanent contents by courts has been, in some instances, explicitly denied by courts. In *ALA Schechter Poultry Corporation v United States*, for instance, the US Supreme Court has declared: 'The Federal Trade Commission Act introduced the expression "unfair methods of competition", which were declared to be unlawful ... We have said that the ... phrase has a broader meaning, that it does not admit of precise definition; its scope being left to judicial determination as controversies arise ... What are "unfair methods of competition" are thus to be determined in particular instances, upon evidence, in the light of particular competitive conditions and of what is found to be a specific and substantial public interest.'[27] The applicability of this standard is determined anew in each and every case: the standard is not replaced by a more determinate rule. For its proposition, *ALA Schechter Poultry Corporation* cited an earlier US Supreme court precedent applying the 'unfair methods of competition' standard. The opinion in that case contained the following footnote:

> The phrase 'unfair methods of competition' was substituted for 'unfair competition' in the Conference Committee. This change seems first to have been suggested by Senator Hollis in debate on the floor of the Senate in response to the suggestion that the words 'unfair competition' might be construed as restricted to those forms of unfair competition condemned by the common law. 51 Cong Record 12145. The House Managers of the conference committee, in reporting this change said, House Report No 1142, 63d Congress, 2d Sess, September 4, 1914, at page 19: 'It is impossible to frame definitions which embrace all unfair practices. There is no limit to human inventiveness in this field. Even if all known unfair practices were specifically defined and prohibited, it would be at once necessary to begin over again. If Congress were to adopt the method of definition, it would undertake an endless task. It is also practically impossible to define unfair practices so that the definition will fit business of every sort in every

---

27 295 US 495, 532; 55 S Ct 837, 844 (1935).

part of this country. Whether competition is unfair or not generally depends upon the surrounding circumstances of the particular case. What is harmful under certain circumstances may be beneficial under different circumstances.'[28]

These claims, made both by a congressional committee and by the US Supreme Court, have proved applicable to a variety of contested classificatory terms, whose obstinate refusal to yield to precise formulations has produced a rich literature on the virtues and vices of such 'loose' legal standards.[29]

Alternatively, Hart's thesis can be interpreted as asserting not that vague and indeterminate terms are *replaced* by more determinate standards, but that courts *expand the core* of such terms – thus making them more determinate. How is such expansion effected? Presumably, through the application of these terms to particular cases: once a binding precedent is set, cases whose facts resemble the facts of the decided case are deemed within the core application of that term. For example, the application of the rule 'no vehicles in the park' to a motorised wheelchair will transform what was once a potentially penumbral case into a core case: when a new wheelchair arrives in the park, it would not open the issue anew. In other words, the 'further official action' (which transforms the previously contested term to a properly determinate legal standard) consists in the slow accumulation of precedent: precedents eliminate the indeterminacy of the term as more and more decisions, regarding previously controversial applications, make clearer and clearer where the law stands.

The problem with this second suggestion is that with *contested terms* it usually remains controversial whether a new case is covered by a previous precedent. There is a crucial difference between terms like 'fairness' or 'reasonableness' and terms like 'vehicle'. In the latter case, but not in the former, people agree about the *essence* of the term; they agree as to *why* instances do or do not fall under the term. With essentially contested terms people pervasively disagree as to why an instance falls inside or outside the term: they disagree as to why a certain action is 'fair' or 'reasonable' even if they agree that it is. People who agree that the death penalty is 'unreasonable' often disagree about why it is. When a court decides that a certain action is 'unreasonable', it articulates a variety of factors or circumstances justifying that decision; but new cases will always lack some of those factors or circumstances, or will always have new ones in addition to those. And since people disagree as to the essence of these concepts – as to what are the important elements in deciding their applicability – the new cases, with their new combination of factors, will raise the question of applicability anew. Terms like 'due care' or 'recklessness' or 'reasonableness' always apply to a

---

28 *Federal Trade Commission v RF Keppel & Bros*, 291 US 304, 312; 54 S Ct 423, 426 (1934).

29 The popular terminology for the distinction between 'contested' legal terms and determinate legal terms is the rule/standard distinction ('rules' standing for legal rules having determinate classificatory terms, 'standards' for those having contested ones). For a representative work, including the association of contested standards with an 'altruistic' ideology, see Kennedy, 1976.

particular combination of factors rather than to a clearly identifiable and potentially recurrent element (like a 'wheelchair'). In order to expand the core, the precedent needs to eliminate this sort of controversy; if it does not, there would be no expansion of the core.

The implications for Hart's thesis

The frequent use of 'essentially contested' terms in legal classifications threatens to marginalise the determinacy of the core in the face of the indeterminacy of the penumbra – a rather obvious point, but one which greatly undermines Hart's thesis. Hart is offering an explanation as to the way in which legal requirements are identified. According to Hart, what the law requires in any given case depends on whether that case falls inside or outside the conventional meaning of the general classificatory terms appearing in the relevant legal rule. That determination, in turn, is a function of conventional linguistic agreement; most cases fall clearly inside, or clearly outside, these linguistic conventions.

But as we just saw, this thesis is wide of the mark in the case of essentially contested concepts: their applications are *not* characterised by agreement but are, instead, the subject of pervasive controversies. It is also a thesis with little explanatory power, as far as essentially contested concepts are concerned, even in those cases upon which people *agree*: to describe the decision as to whether an action is 'reasonable' or 'reckless' as a matter of following a linguistic convention is to miss that entire decision-making process. Sure enough, people do follow a linguistic convention of sorts when applying these terms: people agree about some very abstract and vague formulation of what 'reasonableness' or 'recklessness' are; but they disagree about the content with which these vague formulations are to be fleshed out; they disagree about what these vague formulations actually mean in practice. To claim that people follow linguistic conventions in determining what the law requires is to say very little about that process if that process revolves around the applicability of terms like 'reasonableness', 'good faith', 'recklessness', 'excessive force', 'unfair dealing', 'coercion', 'excessive burden', and many more.

This threat to the significance of Hart's theory of law is at its clearest when one considers Hart's take on judicial impartiality. As we saw, Hart draws a distinction between legal interpretation and judicial legislation. Proper legal interpretation is, presumably, always impartial: to follow linguistic conventions, says Hart, is not to make any real choice but only to refer to a choice already made by the linguistic community. Once the community has settled on what a 'vehicle' means, the idea that a Mercedes Benz is a vehicle is simply a matter of fact. This means that there is no space for considerations of preference to impact legal interpretation so long as legal interpretation is a matter of following linguistic conventions. However, this is untrue in the case of essentially contested concepts: applying a concept like 'reasonableness', even in those applications upon which we agree, is a determination that leaves ample room for considerations of preference. The decision-making process may very well be tainted by partiality even in those cases where people agree about the application. It is for this reason that Hart categorised the application of essentially contested concepts as *judicial legislation* rather than legal interpretation: he says, as we saw, that it is a delegation of rule-making authority to the courts. This, of course, does not solve the problem, but only shifts it to another domain: if the application of essentially contested concepts is judicial legislation rather than legal interpretation, then judicial legislation is much more pervasive than Hart would have us believe. For in that case judicial legislation does not exist only on the 'margins of rules': it exists in *all* the applications of rules containing essentially contested concepts.

Still, Hart's thesis may have an even bigger problem than those posed by essentially contested concepts. Hart's theory may not only prove inapplicable to much legal practice – it may prove inapplicable to all of it.

III   Legal practice and the linguistic boundaries of legal rules

The idea that legal practice consists in the classification of instances as falling within or without general terms in accordance with their conventional meaning doesn't seem right. I will begin the discussion of this simple but fatal defect with a short synopsis of some legal cases, and then examine various responses to the challenge that these cases pose for Hart.

Excluding the included

In *Kaiser Aluminum & Chemical Corporation v Weber*,[30] the US Supreme Court was called to decide whether a private corporation implementing an affirmative action policy, where black employees received preference in admission to a training program, was in violation of Title VII of the Civil Rights Act, which states in a relevant part:

> It shall be an unlawful employment practice for any employer, labor organization, or joint labor-management committee controlling apprenticeship or other training or retraining, including on-the-job training programs, to discriminate against any individual because of his race, color, religion, sex, or national origin in admission to, or employment in, any program established to provide apprenticeship or other training.[31]

The plaintiff was a white employee who had been refused admission to the training program despite his seniority vis-à-vis admitted black employees. The sole reason for his rejection was the affirmative action policies of the employer. The court held that these policies did not violate the statute, ruling that the primary concern of Congress in enacting Title VII was the improvement of working opportunities for blacks, and that it would go against the purpose of the statute to interpret it to forbid the actions of the employer.

---

30 443 US 193; 99 S Ct 2721 (1979).

31 Section 703(d), 78 Stat 256; 42 USC § 2000e-2(d).

In *State v Central Power & Light Corporation*, the state of Texas brought suit against a utility company for its alleged breach of an anti-trust statute.[32] The company entered into an agreement with the City of Yorktown, a municipal corporation, whereby the city agreed to abstain from erecting a power plant in exchange for a sum of money. The suit alleged that the contract was void by operation of a Texas statute prohibiting any agreement between 'corporations' aimed at 'restricting, preventing, or lessening competition in the manufacture, sale, or purchase of any commodity, or to abstain from engaging in or continuing in any business in this State'.[33] The Supreme Court of Texas rejected the claim, holding that a 'corporation' for purposes of this act did not include municipal corporations but only private corporations. The court reasoned that the penalties demanded by the statute are so severe that: 'if the Legislature had intended to visit such severe penalties on municipalities, it would have used more apt language to describe them. Under these circumstances, it is the opinion of the court that the act in question was not intended to include a combination between a municipality and a third party.'[34]

Kingsley v Hawthorne Fabrics, Inc was a New Jersey Supreme Court case involving a tax provision aimed at preventing corporations from paying reduced tax rates on account of owing money to major shareholders.[35] Under that provision, money owed by the corporation to one of its major shareholders or a member of her immediate family was to be included in the calculation of the corporation's net worth. The statute thus provided that the corporation's 'net worth' is the basis for the assessment of the owed tax, and that:

(d) 'Net worth' shall mean the aggregate of the values disclosed by the books of the corporation ... [including] (5) the amount of all indebtedness owing directly or indirectly to holders of 10% or more of the aggregate outstanding shares of the taxpayer's capital stock ...

(e) 'Indebtedness owing directly or indirectly' shall include, without limitation thereto, *all indebtedness owing to any stockholder or shareholder and to members of his immediate family* ...[36]

The case involved a corporation's substantial debt to a business owned by the two brothers of a major shareholder. In assessing the corporation's tax rate the Division of Taxation decided to count that debt as part of the corporation's assets (rather than its debts), reasoning that the debt falls under the provision above. The New Jersey Supreme Court disagreed, ruling that the case does not fall within the statutory provision. The court explained that the provision is relevant only where the members of the said family live under one roof, and

---

32 139 Tex 51; 161 SW 2d 766 (1942).

33 Article 7426, Revised Civil Statutes, 1925.

34 139 Tex 51, 56; 161 SW 2d 766, 768 (1942).

35 41 NJ 521; 197 A 2d 673 (1964).

36 NJSA 54:10A–4(d), (e) (emphasis added).

the statute therefore does not apply to cases where said family members are grown adults having their own households.

Finally, *United States v Kirby* involved indictment brought against a sheriff for violation of a statute providing that: 'if any person shall knowingly and willfully obstruct or retard the passage of the mail, or of any driver or carrier, or of any horse or carriage carrying the same, he shall, upon conviction, for every such offence, pay a fine not exceeding one hundred dollars; and if any ferryman shall, by willful negligence, or refusal to transport the mail across the ferry, delay the same, he shall forfeit and pay, for every ten minutes that the same shall be so delayed, a sum not exceeding ten dollars.'[37] The sheriff arrested a man who was carrying the mail of the United States from the city of Louisville in Kentucky to the city of Cincinnati in Ohio. The arrest came pursuant to a warrant for murder issued against the man. The US Supreme Court quashed the indictment, ruling that Congress had no intention to immunise postal workers from arrests and detentions – particularly 'when the crimes charged against them are not merely *mala prohibita*, but are *mala in se*'![38]

Including the excluded

The excluding of the included has its complement in the including of the excluded. In *Welsh v United States*, the US Supreme Court was faced with an appeal from a conviction for refusing to submit to induction into the Armed Forces.[39] The appeal came to focus on section 6(j) of the Universal Military Training and Service Act, which reads in a relevant part:

> Nothing contained in this title shall be construed to require any person to be subject to combatant training and service in the armed forces of the United States who, by reason of religious training and belief, is conscientiously opposed to participation in war in any form. Religious training and belief in this connection means an individual's belief in a relation to a Supreme Being involving duties superior to those arising from any human relation, but does not include essentially political, sociological, or philosophical views or a merely personal moral code.

Welsh did not belong to any religious group, nor did he adhere to the teachings of any organised religion. In filling out his exemption application Welsh did not sign the statement 'I am, by reason of my religious training and belief, conscientiously opposed to participation in war in any form'; and he did not affirm that he believed in a 'Supreme Being', stating instead that he preferred to leave the question open. He did, however, affirm on the applications that he held deep conscientious scruples against taking part in wars where people were killed. There was no question about Welsh's sincerity and depth of convictions as a conscientious objector, but his application for the exemption was denied on the basis that he was not a religious objector – the Department of

---

37 4 Stat at Large 104.

38 74 US 482, 486; 19 L Ed 278, 279 (1868).

39 398 US 333; 90 S Ct 1792 (1970).

Justice's hearing officer finding 'no religious basis for the registrant's beliefs, opinions and convictions'. Welsh subsequently refused to submit to induction into the military and was convicted of that offence. The conviction was affirmed by a court of appeals.[40] The US Supreme Court reversed the decision, holding that Welsh qualified for the exemption as a religious objector. Stating the issue as 'the serious problem of determining which beliefs were "religious" within the meaning of the statute',[41] the court concluded that the sincerity and depth of Welsh's beliefs, and the central role they occupied in his life, rendered them 'religious' for purposes of the draft exemption statute.

Hart's difficulty

Now for Hart, as we saw, the law is made up of rules having general classificatory terms, and the application of these rules consists in the classification of cases as falling within or without these terms. Legal classificatory terms have, by virtue of being general terms in a natural language, core and penumbral applications. If a case is plainly and clearly subsumed within the classificatory general term of a rule, the case is a plain and clear case for the application of the rule; and if a case plainly and clearly falls outside such general term, then the rule is inapplicable. Yet the cases above all go against this principle: in *Kaiser Aluminum & Chemical Corporation v Weber* the expression 'discriminate because of race' was held not to apply to an employee denied training because of his skin colour; in *State v Central Power & Light Corporation* it was held that a municipal corporation is not a 'corporation' within the meaning of that term; in *Kingsley v Hawthorne Fabrics, Inc* the court ruled that brothers do not fall under the term 'immediate family'; and in *United States v Kirby* a man who knowingly and wilfully retarded the passage of US mail was held to be exempt from the operation of a statute penalising the 'knowing and willful retardation of the passage of US mail'. In *Welsh v United States* the expression 'religious belief' was held applicable to a non-religious belief.[42] Now, shouldn't Hart's theory regard these decisions as *violations* of the law? It would be surprising if it did, but it is hard to see why it is not committed to this position.

Context

One way to avoid this problem is to assert that the applicability of terms is always a function of context: general terms are used in various contexts under varying standards of applicability. The general term 'cat', for example, applies both to the domestic cat and to the family of mammals that includes the lion,

---

40 404 F 2d 1078 (9th Cir 1968).

41 398 US 333, 338; 90 S Ct 1792, 1795 (1970).

42 This is an example where an instance falling clearly outside the ambit of a rule's general classificatory term is nevertheless held to fall within its ambit, so that the 'penumbral' applications of that general term did not define the 'outer' boundaries of the rule's application.

and only context would determine whether an instance falls inside or outside that term. If spoken in a zoologists' conference the term might apply to the Bengal tiger – an application which would be totally wrong in an old lady's living room. Similarly, it is the context which determines whether a brother falls inside the general term 'immediate family', or whether pacifism qualifies as a 'religious belief': and the contexts of the cases above may have meant 'no' for the first question and 'yes' for the second. So these cases fit Hart's principle: it *was* the conventional linguistic meaning of these terms – *determined by the relevant context* – which dictated these decisions.

Now there can be little doubt that, broadly speaking, the 'context' of those cases indeed determined the applicability of those terms; but this 'context' had little to do with the conventional meanings of those terms. In actual fact, the general terms were held inapplicable (or applicable) to their cases because the *rules* were held inapplicable (or applicable) to them – a complete inversion of the causality suggested by Hart, where rules are held applicable or inapplicable to cases because of the applicability or inapplicability of their general terms. If 'context' can include the sort of considerations which motivated those cases' resolutions (the purpose of Congress in enacting Title VII, or the harshness of the punishment prescribed by an anti-trust statute) – and if 'context' determines the applicability of legal classificatory terms – then Hart's theory is wrong from the very beginning.[43]

Legal meaning

A different though related claim is that *legal* terms have different core and penumbral applications from the core and penumbral applications of those terms in everyday language. It is the *legal* meaning against which we should judge the penumbra and the core – whereas my objection relies, erroneously, on the common-language meaning of the classifications. It is the *legal* meaning of the term 'immediate family' that does not apply to one's married brothers, the *legal* meaning of 'racial discrimination' that does not apply to the operation of an affirmative action program, and the *legal* meaning of a 'knowing and willful retardation of mail delivery' which is inapplicable to the arrest of a mail carrier.

---

43 Commenting specifically on the claim that the correct application of rules turns on their *purposes*, Hart says: 'No one has done more than Professor Lon Fuller of the Harvard Law School in his various writings to make clear such a line of argument and I will end by criticizing what I take to be its central point. It is a point which again emerges when we consider *not those legal rules or parts of legal rules the meanings of which are clear and excite no debate but the interpretation of rules in concrete cases where doubts are initially felt and argument develops about their meaning.*' Hart, 1958, p 628 (emphasis added). It is only when the application of the general terms is unclear that 'purposes', for Hart, come to figure in the resolution of cases: 'If it is true that the intelligent decision of *penumbral* questions is one made not mechanically but in the light of aims, purposes, and policies, though not necessarily in the light of anything we would call moral principles, is it wise to express this important fact by saying that the firm utilitarian distinction between what the law is and what it ought to be should be dropped?' Hart, 1958, p 614 (emphasis added).

This response, however, has the following problem: if the standards of applicability of *legal* terms are different from the conventional standards of their non-legal meanings, then why are these standards 'conventional'? One may be tempted to respond that they are conventional because they are shared by the *legal community* – by judges, lawyers, legal academics, or government bureaucrats, though not necessarily by the population at large. This response, however, would not do, and for an obvious reason: if Hart's claim revolves around linguistic conventions shared only by the legal community (and not by the population at large), what is his basis for asserting that such conventions exist? If anything, the 'legal community' shows great divisions regarding the applicability of legal terms. In other words, if it is not the conventions of everyday language which determine what is a core application of a legal general term and what a penumbral application, then the very reason for claiming that the correct application of legal terms turns on conventional agreement disappears. The truth, of course, is that Hart asserted the conventionality of the standards of applicability of legal terms by relying on the presumed conventionality of everyday language. The claim that the conventions of legal terms are not the conventions of everyday language would pull the rag from underneath Hart's theory.[44]

Erroneous legal determinations?

Alternatively, one might try to weather the consequences: the cases above, some might say, are indeed not proper decisions at law: these are errors as far as legal interpretation is concerned. After all, judges do make mistakes! Why assume that this list of cases shows Hart in the wrong and not the deciding judges? The reason why is that such deviations from Hart's thesis are quite common. These cases are not extraordinary exceptions – they are merely very clear examples of the sorts of decisions legal practitioners make all the time. Legal resolutions are not foreclosed by the conventional meaning of legal classificatory terms: the claim that cases falling clearly inside or outside those conventional meanings are clear legal cases is a claim with too many counter-examples. This is a methodological point concerning the nature of theory: if Hart's theory of legal determinations fails to correspond with routine actual decision-making, then Hart's theory must be wrong. If it is admitted that Hart's theory cannot be reconciled with the cases above, then Hart's theory fails to account for too many legal determinations.[45]

---

44 It is for the same reason that one cannot claim that Hart spoke of the conventionality of legal interpretation, rather than the conventionality of legal terms.

45 Ronald Dworkin made a similar point when he claimed that legal positivism does not 'fit' the legal materials. For a discussion of this point, see Chapter 4, section entitled 'The best theory: "fit" and "justification"'.

The majority of cases

In response to all this, one may try a different direction: one may admit that such deviations may indeed be common, but claim that a review of judicial practice will show that in the majority of cases it is the applicability of the general classificatory term which determines the applicability of a legal rule. Hart can then be said to have captured the determinants of legal determinations in *most* cases (and, consequently, to establish the impartiality of legal interpretation for the majority of legal cases), despite the fact that a minority of cases do not follow that pattern.

The question we should ask ourselves, however, is what accounts for the distinction between those cases which accord with Hart's theory and those which do not – the distinction between cases that are disposed of in accordance with the conventional meaning of classificatory terms, and cases that are not. Now if we agree that this distinction is not *arbitrary* – as indeed we must – then Hart's theory must be wrong regarding *all* cases: for this means that a certain judgment *precedes* the decision to follow or not to follow the conventional meaning of the relevant term. In which case it is, at the very outset, that preceding judgment, and the considerations feeding into that judgment, that determine whether a rule is applicable or not, or whether the case is a clear or an unclear case for the law. In that case Hart's theory tells us nothing at all about the measure of legal determinacy, for instance, or the extent and presence of judicial discretion, or any of the other matters which Hart believed he was addressing. The problem with the sort of cases presented above is that they make a point not only about those instances where linguistic conventions are clearly not followed, but also about those instances where they are.[46]

A theory of law, not a theory of adjudication

As a last resort, one may claim that Hart's theory is not a theory of adjudication: Hart does not purport to tell us how judges or other legal interpreters decide cases, but how the law does. This claim makes a distinction between what the law requires, and what judges require when resolving cases. Judges and other legal practitioners – so the claim goes – take into account considerations other than the law in disposing of cases. The rules above were not applied as their language required not because the law requires anything different, but because

---

46 Ronald Dworkin makes a similar argument when discussing his counter-examples to Hart's theory: 'Suppose someone argues against utilitarian theories of justice by showing that these theories fail to explain why slavery is unjust in some actual or imaginary situation in which slavery in fact maximizes utility. He might concede that in other or imaginary situations slavery is counter-utilitarian, but his argument is meant to show that even then slavery is not unjust *because* it is counter-utilitarian. My argument has the same ambition. I appeal to modern complex legal systems to show that since, in these legal systems, the truth of a proposition about legal rights may consist in some moral fact, the positivist conception of legal rights must be a poor one. I conclude that we must abandon the positivist conception in favor of a different conception of the sort I describe.' Dworkin, 1984, p 252.

the judges employed other considerations apart from what the law requires. This is no error on the part of those judges: resolving legal cases involves going beyond what the law requires.[47] Now this seems to me quite an impossible claim to make as far as Hart's theory is concerned – and quite a self-defeating claim as far as legal positivism goes. This claim in effect says that what Hart calls legal rights and duties may be quite different from the legal rights and duties recognised by judges (since judges insist that their decisions reflect what the law requires, nothing less nor more). Apart from the obvious oddity of this claim, it also appears incompatible with Hart's methodology: after all, Hart presumes to tell us what the law requires by observing the actions and declarations of judges. So if judges establish rights and duties which do not follow from the conventional meaning of the classificatory general terms, on what basis can Hart claim that these rights and duties are not the 'real' legal rights and duties? Hart certainly offers no justification for such a strange reading of the evidence. More importantly, according to this reading Hart did not even try to engage with any of the pressing problems of legal theory. That the application of the law revolves around linguistic conventions is not very interesting if legal practitioners habitually recognise legal rights and duties while sidestepping these conventions. In that case there may be little point in fighting over this claim: when the enemy has retreated to the point where it merely occupies its own bases, the battle is to all intents and purposes won. Nevertheless, I will say more about this strategic retreat, because it has proved rather popular.

IV   Legal positivism after Hart

If Hart's thesis fails, then so should his important claims about legal practice. I take the importance of Hart's thesis to reside in the following claims: legal rights and duties (those rights and duties we care about – those that lawyers and judges speak about, and those which the power of the state stands ready to enforce and protect) are identified as a matter of conventions we can all recognise. That process is therefore for the most part non-controversial, and those controversies that do arise are a marginal minority. This thesis, as I said, appears to engage the major problems of modern legal theory: it establishes the impartiality of proper legal interpretation, and it also addresses the grounds of legal determinacy, the distinction between adjudication proper and judicial legislation, the circumstances and extent of judicial discretion, and other related difficulties which occupy modern legal philosophy.

But Hart's theory is wrong: legal determinations are not a matter of applying linguistic conventions. This poses a certain dilemma to legal positivists: they may renounce Hart's exposition, claiming that legal

---

47 For the position that legal interpreters habitually and legitimately decide cases not in accordance with the law's requirements, see, eg, Raz, 1986, p 1,107; Kramer, 1999, pp 149–50; Leiter, 1997, fn 158; Gardner, 2001, pp 211–14.

positivism's fundamental claims can be based on something other than, say, the linguistic conventions of general classificatory terms; or they may try to hold on to Hart's exposition, but let go of his important conclusions. In the event (probably because it is hard to fathom what can replace linguistic conventions in the positivist project), modern legal positivism opted for the second alternative – for theories that stick to some version of Hart's thesis (the correct application of the law *is* a matter of applying linguistic conventions) but drain any real significance out of the claims that his thesis makes.

A theory of law

We have already met one of these theories: the claim that legal positivism is not a theory of adjudication but a theory of law. Judges, says this theory, habitually (and legitimately, as far as legal practice is concerned) override what the law requires and decide cases according to 'extra-legal' considerations. But in that case, as I noted above, legal positivism has nothing to tell us about the way in which legal cases are resolved, about the limits of legitimate judicial discretion, about the determinacy of legal determinations and about all the other issues that constitute the main battlefield for modern theories of law. And if that is the case, our entire set of concerns (over impartiality, determinacy, discretion, and so on) simply extends to these 'extra-legal' considerations that legal interpreters use side by side with the legal ones. After all, it can hardly be doubted that these 'external' considerations admit of certain constraints imposed by the nature of the legal endeavour. Judges cannot legitimately appeal to any consideration they may think of; their decision-making is shaped and guided by the legal context within which they operate.[48] Thus the analysis and understanding of these constraints, and the way in which the 'external' considerations interact with the legal ones, is what legal theory must concern itself with in order to grapple with its significant issues. If legal positivism is limited to what this claim says it is, then legal theory only begins where legal positivism comes to an end.

Soft legal positivism

The second example of positivism's flight to triviality concerns what came to be known as 'soft positivism'. In an article named *Negative and Positive Positivism* Jules Coleman claims that 'the law is everywhere conventional in nature' – even if the legal validity of rights and duties can be a function of controversial moral reasoning![49] The 'conventionality' which Coleman

---

48 In fact, some legal positivists that advance this form of positivism do not deny that. See, eg, Raz, 1972, p 843. ('The thesis of judicial discretion does not entail that in cases where discretion may be exercised everything goes. Such cases are governed by laws which rule out certain decisions. The only claim is that the laws do not determine any decision as the correct one.') But we are then left to wonder what significant information can be derived from this thesis of judicial discretion.

49 Coleman, 1982, p 163.

proclaims is thus very different from the conventionality which secures legal impartiality. Coleman is not shy about what his thesis seeks to achieve: the essential point of legal positivism, he says, is 'to deny what natural law asserts: namely, a necessary connection between law and morality'.[50] This turns legal positivism essentially into a negative thesis: it is reduced to the assertion that there may exist (sometime, somewhere) a legal system whose truth conditions for legal validity have nothing to do with the morality or immorality of the legal proposition in question (with the added proviso that whether things are so is itself a matter of convention).[51] This new version of legal positivism relegates itself to the status of an academic footnote – an argument about the possibilities of possible worlds and the unconventional nature of conventions. It does not even matter whether *soft* legal positivism is or is not a 'theory of law, not adjudication': the possibility of moral (or other controversial) considerations impacting legal interpretation is already granted anyway. Whether legal positivism can defend this modest claim (itself a doubtful question) is hardly a matter of importance: it is sufficient that soft legal positivism tells us nothing whatsoever about legal determinacy, objectivity, judicial discretion, the possibility of impartial legal applications, or any other such question of significance. Where we stand today, legal positivism is a theory that has retreated to virtual irrelevancy.

Post-Hart legal positivism appears to have abandoned the sense of purpose which gave rise to that intellectual movement, and which dominated it for so long.[52] That sense consisted in portraying legal practice as a hard science rather than a malleable art, as objective rather than subjective and, in short, as impartial on account of its methodology.

---

50 Coleman, 1982, p 140.

51 Though, once more, that convention may be very different from the sort of conventionality Hart was defending. For example, the convention that any valid law must not be 'grossly immoral' – no matter how much people disagree about what is or is not 'grossly immoral' – would suffice (according to this thesis) to establish the 'conventionality' of legal practice.

52 The one modern strain of legal positivism which avoids this flight to triviality is normative legal positivism, whose claims are examined in the following chapter.

Chapter 3
Max Weber and the virtues of legal positivism

I Weber's thesis

The previous chapter ended with the claim that what motivated Hart's thesis, and the entire positivist project until its modern retreat, was the wish to portray legal interpretation as an impartial decision-making process. Now this claim may prove controversial even for those who *agree* that traditional legal positivism seeks to present an attractive picture of legal interpretation: after all – so the opposing argument goes – the picture of legal interpretation presented by legal positivism possesses a number of significant virtues apart from any concern with impartiality. This position is directly related to a third strain of contemporary legal positivism (other than the two examined at the end of the previous chapter), which still holds to a meaningful version of that school of thought: *normative* legal positivism. This school offers legal positivism not necessarily as a description of actual legal practice, but as a description of what legal practice *should be*: it views legal positivism as a theory of law having some important qualities which justify its adoption by legal interpreters.[1] In short, according to this position legal positivism possesses a number of important virtues (exclusive of any claim for an impartiality), and the impartiality of legal interpretation therefore need not be positivism's motivating force.

This chapter is an examination of a famous exposition of these virtues. The author of this exposition was not a legal philosopher; but his thesis is a paradigmatic statement of positivism's alleged qualities. The renowned sociologist Max Weber, writing at the turn of the 20th century, advanced a wide-ranging thesis regarding the methodology employed by modern Western law, the relation of this methodology to Western capitalism, and the basis for Western law's claim to legitimacy. According to Weber, the ascendancy of capitalism in the West required a certain 'mode' of legal decision-making – a mode taken straight from the theory of legal positivism. Weber's thesis seeks to link the functional virtues of legal positivism to the functional necessities of the modern capitalist state. Section I of this chapter surveys Weber's claims for the functional virtues of 'formal rational law' (which is Weber's version of legal positivism); section II criticises that thesis; and section III re-examines the relation between impartiality and formal rational law. As will become clear,

---

1   See, eg, Campbell, 1996; MacCormick, 1985; Waldron, 2001.

formal rational law does not possess the virtues that Weber claims for it – though it does describe an impartial methodology of legal interpretation.

Weber's categories of legal thought

What Weber was most interested in explaining was the rise of capitalism in Western Europe, which he saw as a function of the peculiar religious, political, economic, and legal characteristics of Western European society (themselves a result of certain historical conditions found in Europe but not elsewhere). Weber – a lawyer by training – saw European law as a unique phenomenon among the legal systems of the world – a particular form of law which both facilitated, and was facilitated by, the rise of Western capitalism. In elaborating the links between the social, economic, and political phenomena which constitute his thesis, Weber uses his famous methodology of 'pure types': idealised constructions of practices and institutions which do not purport to constitute a faithful representation of any actual specimen, but instead come to highlight some important or essential aspects of those. Thus, while recognising that the real world contains various adulterations and admixtures of these ideal types, Weber seeks to enhance our understanding by articulating certain exemplary features, and then associating these features with a number of (impure) actual examples – in this case, actual legal systems. (Weber's work is so full of examples as to knock unconscious any unseasoned reader.)

In a section entitled 'The Categories of Legal Thought' in his monumental (posthumous) work *Economy and Society*, Weber outlines four types of legal systems – each distinct from the others in its relation to the 'rationality' of the law and to its 'formality'.[2] The different types of legal thought are distinguished primarily by reference to their 'law-finding' methods – that is, their method of legal interpretation – though, as we shall soon see, certain types of legal thought presuppose certain types of legislated laws (certain types of law-finding presuppose certain types of law-making). The first category of law is named 'formal irrational law', and is to be found where 'one applies in law-making or law-finding means which cannot be controlled by the intellect, for instance when recourse is had to oracles or substitutes therefor'.[3] 'Substantive irrational law' is found where legal decisions are 'influenced by concrete factors of the particular case as evaluated upon an ethical, emotional, or political basis rather than by general norms'.[4] Then comes 'formal rational law' (to which modern Western law belongs) where 'only unambiguous general characteristics of the facts of the case are taken into account' in applying the law.[5] This category further divides into two types. The first is

---

2   See Weber, 1978, pp 654–58.

3   Weber, 1978, p 656.

4   Weber, 1978, p 656.

5   Weber, 1978, pp 656–57. It may be worth noting that Weber considered English common law to be different in character from the continental model of formal rationality and closer to the model of substantively rational law.

where 'the legally relevant characteristics are perceptible as sense data. This adherence to external characteristics of the facts, for instance, the utterance of certain words, the execution of a signature, or the performance of a certain symbolic act with a fixed meaning, represents the most rigorous type of legal formalism'.[6] The second type of formal rationality occurs where 'the legally relevant characteristics of the facts are disclosed through logical analysis of meaning and where, accordingly, definitely fixed legal concepts in the form of highly abstract rules are formulated and applied'.[7] Finally, there is the category of 'substantive rational law', where 'the decision of legal problems is influenced by norms different from those obtained through logical generalisation of abstract interpretations of meaning. The norms (or rules) to which substantive rationality accords predominance include ethical imperatives, utilitarian and other expediential rules, and political maxims, all of which diverge from the formalism of the "external characteristics" variety as well as from that which uses logical abstraction'.[8]

Let us improve our understanding of these categories through the use of examples. In formal irrational law the decision in a case may revolve, for instance, around whether the hand of the accused is burned by the fire put to it, or whether the woman thrown into the water sinks or floats. Thus legal thought is 'formal irrational' in so far as it revolves around formal tests whose underlying *modus operandi* is not available to the human intellect, and cases are decided strictly according to these tests. Substantively irrational law is, according to Weber, the law administered by the *Kadi* in Islamic law: the *Kadi* hears a dispute and then arrives at a solution by a process purporting to involve intuition and divine guidance.[9] This form of legal thought does not involve any formal tests; instead, the legal solution depends on a reasoning process that is helped and guided by an almighty God. However, the process is irrational in so far as it is guided by intuition – by implicit and unarticulated (or even unarticulable) factors. Formal rational law of the sense data type can be found where a will would be held *per se* enforceable if it was signed in the presence of two witnesses; while the logical analysis type (the second – and predominantly modern – form of formal rational law) is found where the unauthorised diverting of electricity is held not to constitute 'larceny' because 'larceny' is defined as the unlawful taking of chattel, and electricity, according to the logical analysis of meaning, is not chattel.[10] In other words, formal rational law applies its standards by reference to the *meaning* of the words employed in those standards. It is a form of law employing formal tests, but

---

6   Weber, 1978, p 657.

7   Weber, 1978, p 657.

8   Weber, 1978, p 657.

9   The *Kadi* adjudicates by way of 'informal judgments rendered in terms of concrete ethical or other practical evaluations ...'. Weber, 1978, p 976.

10 This is Weber's own example (Weber, 1978, p 885), taken from an actual decision of the German Supreme Court (29 *Entscheidungen des Reichsgerichts in Strafsachen* 111 and 32 oc 165).

these tests (unlike the test of the woman thrown into the water) are rational. Finally, substantively rational law is the type of law that was presumably administered by tribunals in the ex-Soviet Union: decisions were guided by substantive ideological orientation, in furtherance of that ideology. This is a rational form of decision-making, but a *substantive* rather than a *formal* one.

Given all this, the 'rational' *v* 'irrational' and the 'formal' *v* 'substantive' dimensions of law can be explained as follows. Irrationality pertains, first, to legal decisions made by considerations whose relevance to the resolution of the case is beyond the reaches of the human intellect (the hand of the guilty burns, the witch floats); and also to decisions based on the particularities of a case – decision-making that does not attempt to arrive at *generalisations* that are valid for other similar cases. (The *Kadi* deliberates, but he does not seek any generalisations.) This is what distinguishes substantive irrational law from the substantive rational one: substantive rational law is grounded in *generalisations* applicable not only to the particular case but to other cases as well. So rational law employs legal standards whose relevance to the resolution of the case is apparent to the human intellect, and these standards are generalisations applicable to many cases, not only to a particular one. Neither oracles nor particular emotional or ethical intuitions constitute such standards.

What is the formal/substantive distinction about? Apparently, formal legal thought concerns itself with legal standards which do not require any substantive judgment: the sink/float test, or the presence of two witnesses. Yet according to Weber the logical analysis of meaning is also formal. What marks the line between formality and substance *here*? David Trubek thinks that Weber's formal dimension depends on the extent to which a law employs 'criteria of decision intrinsic to the legal system'.[11] According to Trubek, formality denotes the level of *autonomy* of the law: a law is formal to the extent to which legal thought is autonomous. But autonomous from what? After all, magic and oracles (which may belong to formal law) are employed outside the legal realm as well as within it; and even the logical analysis of meaning must derive its analysis from logical and linguistic understandings which exist, so to speak, independently of the law. It appears that what marks for Weber the *formality* of legal thought is not its independence from any 'real world' considerations, but rather its independence from any *evaluative reasoning*: Weber's substantive law is characterised as requiring such evaluations, whereas his formal law is characterised as precluding them. What is it that makes separation from evaluative reasoning so significant for legal thought? The answer is this: for Weber, the rational formal/rational substantive distinction marks the difference between a law whose application is *predictable* and a law whose application is not.[12]

Weber's thesis is this: capitalism can thrive only in a predictable legal environment – 'capitalistic enterprise', he says, '... cannot do without legal

---

11 Trubek, 1972, p 729.
12 Weber, 1978, pp 880–900.

security'.[13] 'Legal science' – as Weber puts it – reaches proper predictability only in the formal rational form of legal thought. Thus, formal rational law is indispensable for capitalism by virtue of its predictability. In other words, legal positivism is good because legal positivism produces predictable legal requirements; and predictable legal requirements are good because they allow the commercial certainty required for proper economic planning and its efficient execution. Note that this alleged virtue of legal positivism in fact goes beyond the mere functional benefits of economic planning which Weber mentions: legal predictability puts the citizen on notice – it lets the citizen know what can or cannot be done, which is a *moral* virtue; it prevents the infliction of punishment where there is no culpability, and it also enhances the autonomy of the individual, by drawing clear boundaries as to what is legal and what is not.

To the thesis on the link between capitalism and legal predictability Weber adds a second thesis: capitalism, he says, requires a set of policies operating against substantive justice, and delinking ethical evaluation from the law is therefore necessary for the smooth implementation of these policies. Formal rational law is essential for capitalism not only because of its predictability, but also because it separates moral considerations from legal determinations.

As I said, what interests me in Weber's thesis is *not* the accuracy of the claim that modern law employs formal rational legal thought: we already saw that Hart's theory, which is similar to Weber's in its fundamentals, is not an accurate description of our legal practice.[14] What we are interested in here is whether formal rational law – that is legal positivism – really possesses the virtues that Weber believes it does.

---

13 Weber, 1978, p 883. See also: 'The bourgeois interests ... had to demand an unambiguous and clear legal system that would be free of irrational administrative arbitrariness as well as of irrational disturbance by concrete privileges, that would also offer concrete guarantees of the legally binding character of contracts, and that, in consequence of all these features, would function in a calculable way.' Weber, 1978, p 847.

14 Weber himself was aware of some rigorous attacks on what was then known as 'conceptual jurisprudence', which is represented in his idea of formal rationality: he mentions the writings of the school of Free Law (*Freirecht*) – the German equivalent of the American and Scandinavian Realism – and of others who rejected the purported method of formal rationality on both descriptive and normative grounds. However, he does not say much about the substance of these attacks, simply referring to them as the 'ideologies' of lawyers moved by the call for social justice and disgruntled by the dullness of mechanical jurisprudence: 'Status ideologies of the lawyers themselves have been operative in legal theory and practice along with those influences which have been engendered by the social demands of democracy and the welfare ideology of monarchical bureaucracy. Being confined to the interpretation of status and contracts, like a slot machine into which one just drops facts (plus the fee) in order to have it spew out decisions (plus opinion), appears to the modern lawyer as beneath his dignity; and the more universal and codified formal statute law has become, the more unattractive has this notion come to be.' Weber, 1978, p 886.

II Predictability and calculability

Weber believes that capitalism requires a more predictable law than its predecessor systems of economic and social organisation. Why? The answer has to do with the more predictable *environment* that capitalistic ventures require: 'The modern capitalist enterprise', says Weber, 'rests primarily on *calculation* and presupposes a legal and administrative system whose functioning can be rationally predicted, at least in principle, by virtue of its fixed general norms, just like the expected performance of a machine.'[15] The capitalist, in other words, needs to know where she stands: the successful investment of large sums of capital requires a calculable commercial environment, and that calculability is made possible by a predictable law. Formal rational law, says Weber, provides the capitalist with the legal predictability she needs: a law whose operation revolves around the logical analysis of meaning (or, as Hart puts it, around linguistic conventions available to all) is a law whose operation is predictable.

Let us suppose that capitalism indeed requires more calculability than other social and economic regimes, and also suppose that the logical analysis of meaning can produce a predictable law. The problem with Weber's thesis is this: predictable law may fail to deliver *calculability*; and with the logical analysis of meaning as the method of law-finding, the law seems posed to do just that. Calculability would not be delivered by predictable law if that law, although predictable *as law*, produces unpredictable requirements as far as commercial expectations are concerned. Weber's own example of adjudication by means of the logical analysis of meaning provides us with a perfect example of this: 'the layman', Weber tells us, 'will never understand why it should be impossible under the traditional definition of larceny to commit a larceny of electric power.'[16] (The German Supreme Court, as I explained above, found this to be so because larceny was defined in the German Civil Code as the 'unlawful taking of chattel', and electricity, according to the logical analysis of meaning, is not chattel.) Now the capitalist who erected the electrical plant surely calculated on selling the electricity produced for a handsome sum, and did not expect to have it diverted with impunity; indeed it must have been quite a shock to discover that stealing electrical power was not theft under German law. This discovery must have been quite a surprise even if it is obvious and predictable to all those involved that 'electricity' does not fall within the meaning of the term 'chattel'. The problem that this case typifies is not merely that the logical analysis of meaning may *in some cases* fail to produce calculability (because then it may still, on the whole, result in more calculability than other forms of law): the problem is that the logical analysis of meaning may in fact produce, *on the whole*, less calculability than other forms of law, even if we agree that it is more predictable where the establishment of

---

15 Weber, 1978, pp 1,394–95.
16 Weber, 1978, p 885.

legal requirements is concerned. After all, the logical analysis of meaning categorically divorces itself from any concern with the capitalist's expectations and needs, whereas other forms of law may very well take these expectations and needs into account when resolving such cases.

Weber seems to be aware of this simple point. He says, among other things, that:

> The legal concepts produced by academic law-teaching bear the character of abstract norms, which, at least in principle, are formed and distinguished from one another by rigorously formal and rational logical interpretation of meaning. Their rational, systematic character as well as their relatively small degree of concreteness of content easily result in a far-reaching emancipation of legal thinking from the everyday needs of the public. The force of the purely logical legal doctrines let loose, and a legal practice dominated by it, can considerably reduce the role played by considerations of practical needs in the formation of the law.[17]

Weber then rests content with this qualification and does not carry it to its ultimate conclusion: if the logical analysis of meaning is emancipated from the 'everyday needs of the public' then the public (or the capitalist) cannot rely on legal requirements to correspond with expectations regarding its everyday needs. Yet, the capitalist cares about legal predictability *only in so far as it helps him plan his investment of capital*: legal predictability is of no help to the capitalist if its resolutions are surprising where his practical expectations are concerned.

So if predictable law is to result in more calculability for the capitalist, it should not frustrate the capitalist's expectations. Also, it should not produce legal requirements that are *themselves* injurious for calculability. But here, again, the logical analysis of meaning seems posed to do that to a larger extent than alternative forms of legal thought. Here is another example of formal rational law taken from Weber's arsenal: Weber believes that it is formal rational law's 'desire for logical consistency' which produced the result that a lease is terminated by the sale of the land.[18] (Presumably, this was brought about by the fact that a lease, according to the logical analysis of meaning, is a personal contract between lessor and lessee.) Suppose things are so, and also suppose that it is predictable that things are so (as Weber obviously believes). In what way, one might ask, does this predictability of the law translate into the calculability in which the capitalist is interested? The capitalist who leases the land as lessee knows this much: she knows that if her landlord decides to sell the land, her lease will be immediately terminated. What she knows with predictable certainty, in other words, is that she has no predictable certainty as

---

17 Weber, 1978, p 885.

18 'It took some effort, for instance, to prevent the incorporation into the German Civil Code of the principle that a lease is terminated by the sale of the land. That principle had originated in the distribution of social power in Antiquity. However, the plan of taking it over into the new Code was entirely due to a blind desire for logical consistency.' Weber, 1978, p 789.

far as her lease is concerned. (The landlord's calculability, on the other hand, would have been the same whether he knows the lease terminates when he sells or whether he knows it terminates in five years: in both cases he has the certainty of knowing until when his land is leased. So overall calculability is certainly reduced by this legal regime.) Here we have an instance where the logical analysis of meaning produces a predictable legal result which is not surprising as far as its practical consequences are concerned; yet this result may be anything but helpful for the capitalist's future planning. And, once more, the reason why the logical analysis of meaning appears posed to produce more such unfavourable results than some alternative forms of legal thought is that it refuses to engage in any substantive analysis of what can or cannot be detrimental for the capitalist's calculability: it concerns itself strictly with the meaning of isolated words, not with the effect of a resolution or the purpose of the legal rule it applies.

I am not merely saying that predictable law is good for the capitalist only as long as that law is not *anti*-capitalist: that point is obvious. (Clearly enough, if the choice is between a law that is predictable in its prohibition of interest-bearing loans and a law that is unpredictable on that score, the capitalist would be better off under the unpredictable law.) Weber claimed not that capitalism requires capitalist-friendly law, but that it requires law that is very predictable. (Feudalism also requires feudalism-friendly law, but, presumably, that law need not be very predictable.) What I am saying is that predictable law can be bad for the capitalist because it may lack the very virtue for which Weber believes it is functional – that is its contribution to calculability; and when applied in accordance with the logical analysis of meaning, it may reduce calculability even under legislation that is very much pro-capitalist in design. That is to say, the logical analysis of meaning can produce less calculability than other forms of legal thought which are, by stipulation, less predictable. Hence substantive rational law may be, on the whole, less predictable than formal rational law: when a case concerning the termination of leases comes before a court, there may be less predictability that the lease will be held to terminate upon the sale of the land – and also less predictability that it will not. Yet calculability may very well be enhanced here: such uncertain law may allow greater planning and calculability than certain law that undermines planning and calculability by its content. In order to invest in fixture equipment for a factory sitting on leased land, I need to know that that investment will pay off – I need to calculate my investment against its expected returns, taking into consideration the expected cost of my lease. However, my ability to predict the cost of my lease may be greater if the law is uncertain as to whether I can hold on to the lease once the land is sold (rather than if it were certain that I may not): I have more security of tenure (and hence more calculability) because I would not necessarily lose my lease if my landlord decides to sell his land. For me to lose the lease it must also be the case that the new landlord is willing to take the risk of going to court, and, if he takes that risk, he also needs to win it.[19]

Here is another example of a law, pro-calculability in design, proving anti-calculability in application under formal rational legal thought. Consider a 'contract under seal' regime devised to supply the capitalist with certainty in the legal regulation and enforcement of contracts: if an agreement is under seal – which is presumably evidence of deliberation, knowledge of the terms, willingness to be bound by them, and so on – it is *per se* enforceable *with no questions asked* (no questions about the fairness of the agreement, about the parties' bargaining power, their unwritten intentions, or anything fuzzy and unpredictable of that sort). This is a very predictable rule as far as rules are concerned, and it also means to enhance calculability; but under formal rational legal thought it may bring many calculability-reducing results. A calculating capitalist signs a 10-year agreement under seal with a factory, after being shown samples of a higher quality than those that are later delivered to her. As far as the contract is concerned (the description of the items, their cost, and so on), the manufacturer is in full compliance, so that under formal rational law the contractual relations would be enforceable. But that would be anything but conducive to the calculability the capitalist needs: the capitalist needs to count not only on the enforceability of the contract, but also on the quality of products she expects that contract to yield.[20]

According to Weber, the capitalist needs the calculability permitting economic long-term planning, but legal rights and duties can be very predictable without giving the capitalist that needed calculability. The capitalist needs to know that her contract is enforceable – but also that it will not be enforced where her reasonable expectations are defeated; she needs the institution of a corporation to provide security from personal liability – but also the knowledge that her trading partners cannot defraud her with impunity under the corporate shield. But the logical analysis of meaning pays no heed to the concern with calculability: it occupies itself solely with autonomous logical analysis, and it therefore appears posed to produce *less* calculability than, say, substantive rational law guided by capitalist concerns (even if it can produce more predictable *legal* results). The move from the predictability of the law to the calculability that capitalism requires is not as simple or direct as Weber seems to believe.

---

19 There are further complications here: the extent to which the landlord and I can contract around the law. However, this complication does not change the final analysis.

20 This example is different in kind from the two previous ones: with the lease of the land, the unfortunate outcome was, according to Weber, a result of maintaining internal consistency with other land regulations; in the case of the larceny of electrical power, the logical analysis of meaning produced an unfortunate result as far as calculability goes because the stolen property somehow failed to fit the words which the drafters happened to choose; and here the statute produces such an unfortunate result despite the fact that the case did fit these words, this being a matter not of unfortunate choice of words but of unfortunate – if well intentioned – choice of action.

This point is so obvious that it may seem odd that Weber makes the claims that he does.[21] Nevertheless, the intuition that led Weber astray is obvious: Weber has in mind the famous 19th century free market model which sees laws (particularly private law) as the 'rules of the game' within which players seek to maximise their utility. The basic idea is this: economic activity is most efficient when the government limits its role to laying down and enforcing certain clear rules of commercial interaction (contract law, regulation of credit, collection of debts, and so on). The government is thus limited to enforcing the 'rules of the game', and economic actors play the game of economic activity knowing what they can do and what they cannot 'free of irrational administrative arbitrariness as well as of irrational disturbance by concrete privileges', as Weber puts it.[22] So long as the rules of the game are certain, players within the game can rationally maximise their gains; they adapt to the rules and work within or around them so as to best achieve their objectives. Uncertain rules are bound to reduce the rational maximisation of utility by reducing predictability and control. The chess player can work with the rule that pawns march straight, or she can work with the rule that pawns march across; but if it is unclear whether pawns can be marched straight or across, her ability to rationally maximise her aims is seriously compromised – because her ability to calculate is. Weber says that: 'Juridical formalism enables the legal system to operate like a technically rational machine. Thus it guarantees to individuals and groups within the system a relative maximum of freedom, and greatly increases for them the possibility of predicting the legal consequences of their actions.'[23] For Weber there is a direct link between the predictability of the law and the amount of freedom it affords: the more predictable the law, the more freedom one has. To give another analogy, if rocks fall down from the sky in an unpredictable pattern, one's freedom of movement is seriously constrained; but if they fall down in a pre-determined pattern, then they afford a 'relative maximum of freedom': one must avoid the times and places where they fall (hence the 'relativity' of the freedom), but can walk freely anytime and everywhere else. Freedom is maximised thanks to calculability in the same way that efficiency is maximised under a predictable legal regime. This is also true in areas beyond the economic sphere: the citizen knows what he can do and what he cannot, and, free from arbitrary

---

21 This is not entirely true: at one point Weber explicitly acknowledges the potential incompatibility between formal rational law and the calculability the capitalist requires. He says of the rise of the logical analysis of meaning that: 'The consequences of the purely logical construction often bear very irrational or even unforeseen relations to the expectations of the commercial interests. It is this very fact which has given rise to the frequently made charge that the purely logical law is "remote from life" (*lebensfremd*). This logical systemization of the law has been the consequence of the intrinsic intellectual needs of the legal theorists and their disciples, the doctors, ie, of a typical aristocracy of legal literati.' Weber, 1978, p 855. This sentence is in direct contradiction to much else that Weber is saying (Weber's inconsistencies are renowned); but since it does not prevent Weber from pressing ahead with his thesis, we will press ahead with it too.

22 Weber, 1978, p 847.

23 Weber, 1978, p 811.

governmental interference, can pursue his happiness and exercise his autonomy to the best of his ability.

But the inference from the examples of the chess and the rocks does not work in the case of the legal regime and the capitalist's calculability (or the citizen's autonomy). First, in chess there is always an overlap between the requirements of the rules and the sort of moves one expects can be made: the former simply define the latter. There can be no reasonable expectations apart from the expectations produced by the rules. Thus, a predictable set of rules is bound to increase calculability in so far as the player can always correctly predict what she can or cannot do. Not so in the case of legal regulations: laws regulate a world with many rules and expectations existing independently of it, and they may therefore spell rights and duties which people may find highly surprising. Predictable law need not spell predictability for those subjected to it; and where legal thought derives legal requirements from an analysis oblivious to any parallel system of rules and expectations, that possibility may easily become the norm.

Secondly, the analogies of the falling rocks and the rules of chess fail to reflect the real possibilities of legal regulation: the choice between rocks falling unpredictably or predictably, or rules of chess being certain or uncertain, obscure the fact that laws can be very predictable while creating a very unpredictable environment. To use the chess analogy, the choice is not merely between a rule requiring pawns to move straight or across, or a rule which is uncertain about the direction of movement; the choice includes a rule where the permitted direction of movement is determined by the throwing of dice. In the latter case, the rule can be very predictable as far as rules go: in case of a dispute about whether a move accords with the rules, there will always be a predictable and uncontroversial result; but the game the rule creates may be highly incalculable indeed. Legal predictability and one's ability to predict and plan may come apart not only because actors can find legal resolutions surprising (even if they are predictable for the legal professionals examining them), but because predictable legal resolutions can themselves produce highly unpredictable environments – a very real possibility where legal thought concerns itself with abstract semantic constructions (rather than with considerations of commercial stability, or with whether citizens were put on real notice).

In short, Weber's logical analysis of meaning may be very predictable as far as legal resolutions are concerned, but also very damaging for the calculability required by capitalism. Calculability may be better achieved by forms of law whose legal resolutions are (by hypothesis) less predictable; for formal law adamantly refuses to consider either the reasonable expectations of people, or the consequences of its resolutions.

III   The real virtues of legal positivism

Weber's thesis is a misconceived piece of backward engineering – an attempt to account for the rejection of natural law theory and its replacement by legal positivism by means of a direct link between that philosophical development and the historical shift of Western economies towards capitalism. (This is very much in line with Weber's reaction against Karl Marx: Marx sought to portray philosophical and ideological beliefs as mere superstructures – mere rationalisations of conditions and practices whose real determinants are material and economic in nature. Weber rebels against that thesis by portraying ideological beliefs as real determinants of economic conditions and practices.) This is how the separation of law and justice, as well as the claim that law-finding consists in the application of authoritative legal rules by means of following their semantic meanings – those two cornerstones of legal positivism – become, for Weber, important factors in the rise of capitalism in the West. Here is the explanation for Weber's remarkably weak claim that formal rational law effects a break with ethical considerations that is necessary for the successful implementation of capitalist policies. It is rather difficult to see why capitalism relies on a break with substantive justice more than, say, feudalism does (after all, wasn't feudalism involved in a greater denial of substantive justice?); or if it does, why the denial of justice cannot proceed unperturbed with courts employing types of legal thought other than formal rationality. (The Soviet tribunals seemed to have employed *substantive* rational legal thought; but their denial of justice in the name of the great cause certainly did not fall short of the denial of justice that capitalism required.) But Weber simply takes this thesis from the self-understanding of legal positivism, the emerging legal ideology of his age: legal positivism asserts that legal determinations are independent of any moral evaluation, and Weber wishes to claim that this is good for capitalism.

The problem with all this is that it is highly unlikely that the change in legal ideology from natural law to legal positivism reflected any fundamental change in the actual considerations employed by legal decision-making, or in the actual results – even if it did manage to carry away, on some unusual occasion, several judges of a European supreme court (perhaps unsurprisingly, a German court):[24] anecdotal cases of this sort are the exceptions which testify for the rule – as the professional outcry that followed that case showed.[25] Weber's mistake consisted in taking the claims of legal positivism far too seriously.

Legal positivism has been a widely accepted philosophy of law for quite some time now, but it was never a good description of legal decision-making.

---

24 I am referring here to the decision that stealing electricity is not punishable by law because electricity is not 'chattel'.

25 Roth and Wittich tell us that the decision became 'the stock "horrible" in modern German excoriations of conceptual jurisprudence'. Weber, 1978, p 897 (fn 13).

But what, then, makes it so popular? If neither putting citizens on notice nor promoting long-term planning and calculability can be served by the form of legal interpretation that legal positivism defends, what is so wonderful about legal positivism? What is so wonderful under legal positivism is, first and foremost, the neutrality of the legal profession and the courts: it presents adjudication as impartial, discretion as tightly controlled, judicial power as largely nominal, and the 'science of law' as an objective skill and not a subjective art. Following the semantic meaning of legislated rules renders the judiciary a mere medium through which legal orders are transferred to their subjects. In such circumstances, there could be no serious concerns regarding the subjectivity of legal interpretation, the extensiveness of judicial discretion, or the alleged undemocratic nature of judicial power – for there is no judicial power of which to speak. The judge who establishes legal requirements through the 'logical analysis of meaning' ('like a slot machine into which one just drops facts ... in order to have it spew out decisions',[26] as Weber so candidly puts it) does not possess any power of his own but merely carries through the power of others (those making the law). The chief virtue of legal positivism remains its portrayal of legal practice as impartial.

---

26 Weber, 1978, p 886.

Chapter 4
Dworkin and the proper methodology of legal theory

I Dworkin's methodological claims

Ronald Dworkin has been one of the chief critics of legal positivism, deserving of much credit for positivism's recent abandonment of its more significant claims. The two following chapters examine Ronald Dworkin's own theory of law. That theory is divided into two parts: a methodological theory, and a substantive proposal. The methodological theory makes claims about a set of assumptions that legal theorists must employ when developing theories of law; the substantive proposal employs the assumptions described in the first part in developing such a theory. This chapter examines Dworkin's methodological claims.

On first blush, these claims appear to contradict the idea that Dworkin is defending the impartiality of legal interpretation. Dworkin asserts, in clear and strong terms, that legal interpreters must develop a theory of law as a prelude to any legal determination, and that this task requires them to make *moral and political* evaluations! If such is the case, how can Dworkin defend the impartiality of legal interpretation? Yet these claims are joined by some other assertions which, together, amount to a defence of impartiality. The examination of Dworkin's claims, their defence of impartial legal interpretation, and the ultimate merit of that defence, proceed as follows: section I explains Dworkin's methodological claims and his basis for making them; section II examines how Dworkin's methodology seeks to defend the impartiality of legal interpretation (through an ancillary thesis); section III examines the merit of Dworkin's methodological claims, concluding that these claims must be rejected; and section IV concludes by summarising both the failings of Dworkin's methodological theory and the insights that it contains.

Dworkin and the problem of essential contestedness

Dworkin's celebrated *Law's Empire* is launched with a rejection of the claim, made by legal positivism, that legal requirements are determined by criteria shared among legal practitioners (that is, by conventions).[1] Legal practitioners, says Dworkin, habitually disagree about which claims or propositions are legally valid, and about why they are: there are no shared criteria to be found

---

1 Dworkin, 1986.

here.[2] Yet if the question of what counts as a legally valid claim is not a question about conventions, what kind of question is it? Dworkin's answer is this: it is a question about the best theory we have of what legal practice is about. The determination of what is and what is not legally valid is settled by appealing to the best theory of law we can get our hands on. This, says Dworkin, is what *interpretive practices* (of which legal practice is one) are about. When we are called to decide whether a certain conduct is or is not *courteous* – courtesy being another interpretive practice – our decision turns on the best available theory of what 'courtesy' is; and similarly, when we decide whether a certain proposition is or is not *legal* we turn to the best theory of what 'law' is. People hold different – indeed incompatible – understandings of these practices; and the true conception is the best one among those.

So what makes a conception 'best'?

The best theory: 'fit' and 'justification'

How are we to evaluate the merit of a conception? Dworkin's test employs two dimensions: 'fit' and 'justification'. Our best conception of an interpretive practice is the conception that best *fits and justifies* that practice. The dimension of fit is self-evident: to say that a conception must fit the practice is to say that it must account for many aspects of the practice generally believed to belong to that practice. For example, in order to be a good conception of the practice of courtesy, a conception must account for many – though not all – of the actions people consider to belong to the practice of courtesy (for instance, opening doors for people, or pouring drinks for others before filling one's own glass).[3] A conception of courtesy claiming that courtesy is a matter of paying homage to old age would presumably fail, because it cannot account for all those numerous instances generally believed to belong to the practice which have nothing to do with old age. There cannot be too many instances which a theory of the practice leaves unaccounted for: a theory presenting itself as an interpretation of a certain phenomenon cannot leave much of that phenomenon outside its scope. Dworkin puts this point in the following way: an interpretation 'must fit enough [of the practice] for the interpreter to be able to see himself as interpreting that practice, not inventing a new one'.[4]

---

2 See Dworkin, 1986, pp 1–44. Dworkin articulates this complaint by opposing what he regards as legal positivism's misconceived semantic assumption: he claims that the concept of law is an 'interpretive concept' – a concept whose correct use is not a function of shared criteria (as the positivists presumably believe). The move to this linguistic perspective is best understood by seeing the interpretation of legal practice as equivalent to the 'conception of the concept of law'. (This equivalence may be most simply understood by seeing the use of the concept of law as the practice being interpreted.) I will stay away from this linguistic perspective: Dworkin's claims can be understood in full, and with more clarity, without it.

3 Dworkin says that an interpretation needs to fit 'the raw behavioral data of the practice'. Dworkin, 1986, p 52.

4 Dworkin, 1986, p 66 (footnote omitted).

A conception does not need to fit *all* those instances generally believed to belong to the practice: the very possibility of formulating a coherent conception may require that not everything fit in. A good conception of courtesy may fail to fit the practice of taking people's shoes off, even if people consider this the highest of courtesies.[5] (Perhaps courtesy properly understood does not encompass acts perceived as subservient.) A conception of a social practice is not shown to be wrong by failing to account for *all* those instances or features commonly believed to belong to that practice. If I claim that marriage consists in a commitment to a long-term relationship, then a demonstration that certain marriages lack such a commitment does not prove me wrong. Theories in the social sciences may categorise instances as abnormal deviations – or simply as wrong. (A theory of legal interpretation may conclude, for example, that certain judicial practices constitute a departure from legal interpretation properly understood; that they constitute an error as far as proper legal interpretation is concerned; that they are not really instances of legal interpretation, even though they are generally believed to be.) Conceptions of social practices seek to pinpoint the *essential* features of those practices, and they may make claims about what instances belong (or do not belong) in the practice by virtue of these instances possessing (or lacking) the identified essential characteristics. Thus, they must fit some, but not all, those instances considered a part of the practice.

The second dimension of Dworkin's test – 'justification' – consists of 'putting the practice in its best light'. A conception of an interpretive practice, says Dworkin, must make the practice 'the best it can be'.[6] What does Dworkin mean by that? What kind of excellence are we talking about here? The best conception, says Dworkin, must show the practice as *worthy of being pursued*, as *desirable* rather than deplorable, as being *good* – and the more worthy or desirable or good it is, the truer our conception.[7] (Indeed Dworkin sets his entire chapter on interpretation in *Law's Empire* as a response to the objection

---

5 In fact, there is some disagreement as to whether a conception may fail to account for instances that are considered *paradigmatic* by the relevant community. On this point, see Endicott, 1998.

6 Dworkin, 1986, p 53.

7 Dworkin, 1986, pp 421–22. At times Dworkin refers to the best light as a requirement of *intellectual* excellence: for example, he draws a parallel between his criterion of best light and the famous principle of charity. See Dworkin, 1986, p 53. Nevertheless, there can be no doubt that Dworkin also has in mind a requirement of *goodness* or *desirability.* He says, for example, that a critic who offers an interpretation of a work of art portraying that work as banal – art being another interpretive practice – will be offering a successful interpretation only if it is assumed that a more attractive interpretation is not available. See pp 421–22 (fn 12). (See also pp 60–61 for the discussion of the debate about author's intention in works of art.) He also says (p 67) that an interpreter assessing whether the practice of courtesy is a matter of showing respect to people of higher rank must make 'judgments about whether social ranks are desirable or deplorable'. Or (p 150) that a correct conception of legal practices would 'justify these practices by providing an attractive picture of law's point'. Dworkin believes, of course, that there is a link between the intellectual excellence of a conception of law and its desirability. Whether such a link actually exists – and where it may come from – is the subject matter of this discussion.

that 'interpretation tries to show the object of interpretation … as it really is, not as you suggest through rose-colored glasses or in its best light'[8] – the response being that interpretation *does* seek to portray its object as the most desirable – as the rosiest – but this in fact shows it as it really is.) Of course, not all interpretations of interpretive practices are geared towards the same desirability: the interpretation of a literary work is geared towards a desirability that is rooted in the artistic literary domain, whereas the interpretation of legal practice is geared towards desirability that is rooted in the realm of political morality.[9] Nevertheless, to put a practice in its best light is to portray it as the most *desirable*; and the best interpretation of an interpretive practice must put that practice in its best light.

Equipped with the twin requirements of fit and justification, the interpreter sets about her job by theorising the *purpose* served by the social practice whose conception she seeks. The interpreter need not look for a purpose that all practitioners have in mind when undertaking the practice (practitioners may disagree about what that purpose is); but the interpretation must hypothesise a purpose – as vague and abstract as may be – because certain inquiries seeking to understand social practices, including the kind of inquiry undertaken by legal philosophy, must approach their subject matter by seeking to understand the *purposes* or *functions* those practices serve.[10] We can, of course, seek to understand social practices *without* recourse to their purposes or functions: we may understand them in certain behaviourist terms, for example, restricting our efforts to the attempt to formulate generalised rules of behaviour along the model of the natural sciences (which speak the language of regularities rather than the language of purposes). But then our interpretation would move away from an entire realm of meaning – the realm of meaning to which legal philosophy belongs. The positing of a purpose, says Dworkin, whether done explicitly or implicitly, is the *'formal* structure' that any jurisprudential interpretation must have.[11] (This claim, I might add, seems to merit no controversy.) In short, the true conception of an interpretive practice is its best conception; and that best conception is the one which best fits the practice and puts it in its best light while hypothesising its purpose.

---

8 Dworkin, 1986, p 54.

9 'Constructive interpretation is a matter of imposing a purpose on an object or practice in order to make it the best possible example *of the form or genre to which it is taken to belong.'* Dworkin, 1986, p 52 (emphasis added).

10 'We must', says Dworkin, 'notice Gadamer's crucial point, that interpretation must *apply* an intention'. Dworkin, 1986, p 55 (original emphasis) (footnote omitted). See also 'the interpretation of social practices … is *essentially* concerned with purposes rather than mere causes'. Dworkin, 1986, p 51.

11 Dworkin, 1986, p 52 (original emphasis). It is therefore a mistake to do as some scholars have done and attack Dworkin for *assuming* that the purpose of law is the justification of state coercion (a claim examined in the next chapter). That hypothesis is itself the structure that Dworkin's own conception assumes: rather than standing outside and conditioning his conception, it is already the articulation of his own substantive interpretation.

Why best light?

Now why must the true conception of legal practice put it in its best light? Why can't the true conception of legal practice put it in a *bad* light? According to some critical scholars, the determination of legal rights and duties revolves around whether those rights or duties serve the interests of certain economic elites (a conception which seems to put legal practice in a rather bad light). Why is a conception showing legal practice in a more desirable light (assuming an equal level of fit) more *true*, by that fact alone, than the conception advanced by these critical scholars?

The answer to this question begins with the claim that legal practitioners seek to put legal practice in a desirable light when making legal determinations.[12] We expect the reasons for which a claim is recognised as legally valid to entail the worthiness of legal practice, not its wickedness. It sounds crazy for a judge or a lawyer to suggest that a legal claim is legally valid on grounds that this serves the interests of the rich: practitioners employ a *desirable* conception of the practice when making their legal determinations – not a wicked conception. If legal practitioners understand legal validity to be a function of desirable conditions, and they are the ones who make determinations of legal validity, it follows that any true understanding of the practice's conditions of legal validity must be desirable.

Now this claim seems clear enough (even though it is false); but it does not address the following difficulty: even if we grant that practitioners' own understanding means that a true conception of legal practice need present the practice as desirable, still it remains unclear why – as Dworkin claims – the true conception need present legal practice as the *most* desirable.

The 'most' desirable conception

By virtue of what can such a claim – that the true conception of legal practice is the most desirable – be true? What can be the explanation for it? The claim seems to rest on the following suggestion: practitioners do not merely employ a desirable conception of legal practice when making legal determinations; they employ the *most* desirable conception of it. For them legal practice just *is* the best thing it can be. This would be the case, for example, if practitioners would change their legal determinations when presented with different determinations flowing from a more desirable account of legal practice.[13] This

---

12 Indeed, this is also the reason why, as Dworkin claims, interpretations of works of art putting them in a good light would ordinarily seem more correct than interpretations showing them as banal. An interpretation showing the work as banal or stupid would seem less correct than an interpretation showing the work as sophisticated or smart to the extent that the artist tried to be sophisticated and smart and not banal and stupid.

13 The idea, of course, is not that practitioners choose the most desirable legal rights and duties: X is not legally valid to the exclusion of Y simply because X is more desirable than Y. The claim is that X is legally valid to the exclusion of Y if the *conception of legal practice* (that is, the account of what makes a legal claim true or correct) from which it derives is a more desirable account of legal practice than the conception from which Y derives.

suggestion engages the way practitioners practise their practice – it claims that practitioners practise law in accordance with the most desirable conception of law available to them; they identify the rights and duties flowing from the most desirable conception of law in making the determination that 'such and such is the law'. This is the 'interpretive attitude' which Dworkin attributes to practitioners of 'interpretive practices': practitioners adopt the interpretive attitude when they determine the correct moves within the practice by seeking the most desirable account of that practice.[14] Legal practitioners seek the most desirable conception of legal practice when making legal determinations.

This is why a conception putting legal practice in a *bad* light is for Dworkin a declaration that *we can do nothing better* with it. Dworkin does not rule out the possibility that the true conception of legal practice is unhappy; but he insists that an unhappy conception must demonstrate why a better conception *cannot* constitute the practice: 'The internal sceptic [that is, the one offering an unhappy interpretation] must show that the flawed and contradictory account is the *only one available*';[15] an unfavourable interpretation succeeds only if there is 'no [other] more favourable interpretation [which] fits equally well'.[16] To repeat, this heavy burden with which Dworkin saddles critical interpretations of legal practice is supposed to arise from the fact that practitioners employ the most desirable interpretation available to them when making legal determinations. The demand that a critical interpretation demonstrate the unavailability of an equally fitting but more desirable conception is the other side of this coin.

It is this understanding which underlies Dworkin's belief that 'the contribution that a philosopher can make to political morality really is distinctive': the conceptions (interpretations) developed and made available by philosophers for practices like law or democracy may determine what these practices really are. This picture has also much to do with Dworkin's famous doctrine of the continuity of legal theory and practice – the idea that 'jurisprudence is the general part of adjudication, silent prologue to any discussion at law': legal theory (jurisprudence) develops conceptions of law which in turn determine legal rights and duties. Since there is no conventional understanding regarding what makes a claim legally correct, practitioners must resort (whether explicitly or implicitly) to theory construction in determining the content of law. Legal theory is a philosophical discipline which, in effect, shapes its own subject matter: 'Interpretation folds back into the practice, altering its shape, and the new shape encourages further reinterpretation, so the practice changes dramatically, though each step in the

---

14 Practitioners of interpretive practices, says Dworkin, do not determine what the practice requires 'mechanically'; they do this, instead, by trying 'to impose *meaning* on the institution – to see it in its best light – and then to restructure it in the light of that meaning'. Dworkin, 1986, p 47 (original emphasis).

15 Dworkin, 1986, p 274 (emphasis added).

16 Dworkin, 1986, p 422 (fn 12).

progress is interpretive of what the last achieved.'[17] The best light requirement derives from a thesis about the way practitioners determine what is required by their practice, coupled with the truism that their determinations shape and determine the character of the practice.

II Objectivity, truth, and impartiality

I said that Dworkin – like the positivists he attacks – is committed to defending the impartiality of legal interpretation. Yet from what we have seen so far, Dworkin's methodological claims seem to make impartiality altogether impossible: if legal interpretation necessarily involves an evaluation of what's a *desirable* conception of law (as we saw, legal interpreters must first arrive at a desirable conception of law from which they then derive their legal determinations) then the use of moral preferences appears inescapable. But to his methodological assertions Dworkin adds another thesis – a thesis which purports to take away our concern over moral evaluations: moral determinations, says Dworkin, have one right answer! They are either correct or incorrect! Our fear, as Dworkin understands it, is that legal interpreters use considerations whose choice is in principle unjustifiable (mere 'preferences'); but according to Dworkin, determinations concerning the desirability of legal conceptions *are* either true or false: the choice among them is always justified or unjustified as a matter of principle. The assessment of greater or lesser desirability is as much 'true' or 'false' – says Dworkin – as any empirical claim.

The argument for this claim, put forward in a series of articles, is essentially this: to say that judgments of morality cannot be 'true or false' or are not 'objective' (or cannot be justified 'as a matter of principle') is to use the notion of 'objectivity' or the notion of 'truth' in an odd and unintelligible manner.[18] In fact, saying of a moral proposition that it is 'really true' or 'objectively correct' comes, properly understood, as a mere emphasis to the claim that we believe in such a proposition and we find it persuasive.[19] The truth of a proposition is a function of the strength of the arguments supporting it: if the claim that slavery is morally wrong is supported by good moral arguments, then slavery is indeed truly and objectively wrong. End of story. It is silly to think that the choice among moral propositions is 'in principle unjustified': some moral propositions are better supported than others, and that is all that is needed in order to justify 'in principle' any proposition. So according to Dworkin, there are correct and incorrect moral propositions, and hence correct or incorrect evaluations of the desirability of a conception of law. What legal theory finds

---

17 Dworkin, 1986, p 48.

18 See, eg, Dworkin, 1996; Dworkin, 1985.

19 '[T]he most natural reading of all of the further claims [that a moral view on abortions is "really true", "objective" and so on] shows them to be nothing but clarifying or emphatic or metaphorical restatements or elaborations of the ... proposition that abortion is wrong.' Dworkin, 1996, p 5.

so disturbing in the use of preferences is that legal interpretation might employ considerations whose direct opposites might have been employed just as legitimately. But as far as choosing desirable legal conceptions is concerned, Dworkin claims that such choices are never a mere matter of preference.

However, this does not yet solve our problem, given some foundational modern thought involving the notion of 'value pluralism' – the idea that there are various moral values, and that moral determinations often involve equally valid compromises among those (for example, giving up some liberty in order to gain in equality, or giving up equality in order to gain in liberty).[20] Value pluralism implies that different and incompatible conceptions of law may be equally desirable, for they may represent different compromises of values the choice among which cannot be itself correct or incorrect (one conception privileges equality to the detriment of liberty, the other does the reverse). The reason why moral determinations are often a matter of preference is that it may be a matter of preference whether to privilege one value or another.[21] (In other words, deciding which moral position is better supported by arguments may still be a matter of preference.) Dworkin's response to this potential problem is quite remarkable: he simply asserts his belief in *value monism* – the idea that human values are all interdependent in such a way that an optimal moral determination may maximise *all* values (rather than comprise one possible compromise among them).[22] In other words, according to Dworkin there is always an optimal moral determination which is uniquely true and correct.[23] Specifically to our point, the question of which conception of law is the most desirable has one correct answer.

I will not get into a critical examination of Dworkin's claims regarding the meaning of 'objectivity' or 'truth' (though they seem to me wrong), nor of his value monism. (An examination of whether Dworkin's claims, *even if true*, would alleviate the concern regarding impartiality is undertaken in Chapter 5, below.) I mention Dworkin's claims in order to show that Dworkin is obviously concerned with the impartiality problem, and that he is anxious to show how his theory avoids it. Dworkin's claims regarding the moral evaluations which legal practitioners must undertake in making their legal determinations are seconded by claims regarding the objectivity (hence, potential impartiality) of such moral determinations. Dworkin's concern with

---

20 'Value' refers to something which is desirable as an end in itself, not merely as a means to another thing.

21 It is not very significant, of course, that moral determinations are either true or false if incompatible moral determinations can all be true: Dworkin clearly intends his thesis to guarantee that no two incompatible moral determinations can be correct – and that no two incompatible conceptions of law can be equally desirable. If incompatible moral determinations can all prove to be 'true' then the choice among competing conceptions of law might, after all, be a matter of pure preference.

22 See 'Hart's Postscript', paper presented at Oxford University HLA Hart Lecture Series, 2000.

23 Isaiah Berlin repeatedly characterised similar positions as the discredited philosophical remnants of a previous age. See Berlin, 1990.

the issue of preferences will become even clearer in our examination of his substantive theory of law.

The following section returns to the best light requirement, and to whether the arguments supporting it are at all sustainable (whether evaluations of desirability are a matter of preference or not).

III The problems with relying on practitioners' own understanding

Do practitioners associate legal validity with the desirability of legal conceptions?

The first objection to the best light requirement is that the desirability or undesirability of the conception of law underlying a legal claim is of no importance to practitioners assessing its legal validity. This objection, however, appears to be false: there is much that is true and insightful in Dworkin's claim. Consider, for instance, the argument underlying the spectacular rise of the law and economics movement. Here a group of scholars began claiming that private law is best read as a scheme aimed at maximising economic efficiency, and that the correct legal requirements are therefore derived from such economic considerations. The claim was not framed in terms of what the law *should be*; the claim was framed as a thesis about what the law *is*: about what the correct legal rights and duties are – not what they ought to be. Yet despite the novelty of the claim (the doctrines and precedents upon which the claim was based, apart from some isolated exceptions, seemed to have paid little heed to economic considerations)[24] it was nevertheless quickly accepted by a large number of people. Lawyers, scholars, and judges soon began to claim that the content of the law was this or that because that content flowed from the conception of law as a scheme aimed at maximising economic efficiency: academic articles, court briefs, and judicial opinions all moved through the motions of economic efficiency in purporting to determine legal rights and duties. Now what can explain the success of the law and economics movement?

It is clear that the acceptance of this radical reinterpretation of private law was at least in part motivated by its promise to convert a notoriously problematic legal domain – with its persistent feel of moral subjectivity – into the (purportedly) technically dispassionate realm of economic calculations. What legal practitioners found so attractive in the economic analysis of tort law – above and beyond the obvious attractions of economic efficiency – was the idea that legal resolutions could turn 'objective': that judges no longer needed to dabble in the murky waters of 'negligence', 'reasonableness', or 'due

---

24 The most famous of these exceptions being Learned Hand's economic formulation of tortious negligence in *United States v Carroll Towing Co*, 159 F 2d 169 (2d Cir 1947). This case is credited with giving rise to the law and economics movement.

care'; that instead they could engage in the dispassionate calculations of information costs and self-insurance in making their legal determinations. Now the drive towards an 'objective' legal interpretation is a paradigmatic example of the drive towards a desirable conception of law. Hence, the law and economics movement rose to success thanks to the fact that legal practitioners consider the desirability of a conception of law as important to questions of legal validity.

Note, however, that nothing has yet been said about what *in fact* determines legal validity. Practitioners may very well consider the desirability of a conception of law as important to questions of legal validity; but this need not mean that desirable conceptions of law are indeed the real determinants of their determinations. The law and economics movement may have been successful not only because it presents a desirable conception of law, but also because the economic analysis of law can somehow yield desired legal determinations – that is, determinations which are desirable for reasons having little to do with law and economics' desirability as a conception of law.

The gap between the desirable conception and the actual determination

We can accept the claim that practitioners consider the desirability of a conception of law as important to questions of legal validity; but we may still reject the best light requirement by disputing – along with quite a number of legal scholars – the determinative power of practitioners' own understanding. Many of these legal scholars reject the claim that legal rights and duties are determined by practitioners' desirable conceptions of legal practice; these desirable conceptions, they say, are mere superstructures: remove them and legal determinations will remain as they are. To return to the claim I voiced above – it may be true that no judge would suggest an undesirable conception of law as the standard for evaluating the validity of a legal claim; but so what? An undesirable conception is precisely what it comes down to when legal determinations are in fact made. The claim that 'X is legally valid by virtue of it being good for the rich' sounds crazy only because the judge tells herself – or others – some vacuous story with no real determinative power in the matter. In fact, a close analysis will show that this cover story changes all the time whereas the *real* – and stable – determinant is (say) hopelessly class-oriented. Besides, the suggestion that it is by virtue of serving the rich that a right or a duty is legally valid sounds much less crazy if we move it from the courtroom to a lawyer's office: 'this' – says the lawyer – 'is what I believe to be the law governing this case, for the courts have consistently shown themselves on the side of the rich in this matter'.

What is being disputed here is the causal link between practitioners' desirable conceptions of legal practice and the determinations they make. Dworkin seems to assume that because a certain legal discourse – the 'adjudicative discourse', the sort of discourse heard in the courts – purports to derive legal resolutions from the most desirable legal conception, then legal determinations in fact flow from such a conception. It is precisely this assumption that many critical conceptions dispute: they do not deny that legal determinations are supposed to derive from desirable conceptions of law; they just deny that this is in fact the case.

The account of this disconnection between official discourse and the determinations actually made takes many forms. The crudest accounts suggest that legal practitioners purporting to derive their decisions from desirable legal conceptions simply operate in conscious bad faith: they know that their decisions are determined by some less desirable understanding of their job, but they present them as if they flow from a desirable legal conception. They 'play the game' while simply making the determinations they consider the most moral, or the most efficient, or what have you. When these determinations accord with the 'black letter law', judges present them as dictated by a positivist conception of law; but when they don't accord with the letter then these judges mumble about the 'spirit of the law' and forget all about positivism.[25] Others suggest that legal practitioners are engaged in self-deception: they deceive *themselves* into believing that their decisions derive from considerations which are in fact grafted upon a decision after it has been taken. They simply deny to themselves the realities of their decision-making. Or they may simply be mistaken about their own decision-making processes: self-deception implies a measure of wrongdoing, but legal practitioners may be utterly unaware of the reasons that *really* propel them. Perhaps a careful analysis may grasp these realities better than those practitioners do.

These various claims are supported through different strategies. Some critiques seek to challenge the determinative power of the desirable discourse by demonstrating its indeterminacy *as a discourse*. If the economic considerations identified by economic legal analysis (information costs, self-insurance costs, and so on) are in fact indeterminate, then the economic analysis of law may not be the determinative factor in making legal determinations: if it can be shown that the economic analysis of law can yield conflicting results, depending on the factors one's analysis privileges, and the choice among those factors cannot be itself the result of economic theory, then something other than economic considerations may (indeed *must*) be determinative as to the ultimate resolution. And then it is a further possibility that these real determinants constitute some systemic, analysable, and potentially undesirable pattern which a critical conception of law can expose. The legal realists attacked what they called 'legal formalism' by maintaining that the determinants purporting to guide legal decision-making according to this conception were too indeterminate to yield the resolutions they purported to determine. Judges made legal determinations they purported to deduce analytically from highly abstract legal concepts ('the freedom of contract', for example, or the concept of a 'corporation'); but such concepts cut in too many ways to decide, by themselves, the cases they were proclaimed to decide.[26] The

---

25 So these 'bad faith' explanations do not challenge the importance of practitioners' self-understanding, only what that self-understanding is.

26 See, eg, Cohen, 1935. For a modern example of this sort of criticism, see Gordon, 1987.

real determinants, said some legal realists, were in fact ideological: right wing pro-business judges masked determinations guided by an anti-labour ideology by purporting to use a determinate and desirable – but in fact an indeterminate and undesirable – conception of law.

Others – like law and economics scholars – argue that the (desirable) official discourse is not the determinative one by purporting to uncover a pattern which, they say, better explains legal determinations. Many legal determinations in tort and in contract law are aimed at maximising economic efficiency – despite the fact that practitioners habitually justify them on different grounds altogether. Tort doctrines such as necessity, contributory negligence, or multiple tortfeasors were reinterpreted in terms wholly different from those in which they were originally introduced and discussed – implying that the explicit discourse employed by those introducing them was not the determinative one: rather, it was economic efficiency which determined things all along. Other critical scholars seek to demonstrate contradictions among the considerations figuring in the desirable discourse, thereby implying that these considerations are not the *ultimate* determinants: if the desirable discourse encompasses contradictory considerations, then the desirable discourse cannot really determine the resolution, and the action lies in the factors determining the choice among these contradictory alternatives.[27]

In short, the fact that practitioners consider the desirability of a conception of law as important to questions of legal validity need not mean that legal determinations in fact flow from any desirable conception. And once it is acknowledged that there may be no causal link between practitioners' understanding of the practice and their legal determinations, there seems to be no basis upon which to claim that desirability is at all a criterion of evaluation for the true conception of law.

Ronald Dworkin, Peter Winch, and practitioners' own understanding

In an unpretentious little book, written in 1958 and still going strong, Peter Winch quarrels with the idea that the correct understanding of a social practice may differ from practitioners' own understanding of it.[28] Winch attributes the idea to certain positivist thinkers – Max Weber, Emile Durkheim, and Vilfredo Pareto, among others – who believed that the social sciences must 'get empirical', and must strive to explain human behaviour in scientific terms – which may be very different from the terms employed by the people whose behaviour they seek to explain.[29] Against this Winch asserts that in order to

---

27 See, eg, Ford, 1994; Kennedy, 1976. Here, in contrast to the 'indeterminacy strategy' examined above, the critic often traces the sources of indeterminacy to endemic and unsolvable contradictions.

28 Winch, 1990.

29 It is debatable to what extent this claim is applicable to Weber, who saw the self-understanding of the practitioners of a social practice as an integral part of its social understanding, so that sociology, according to Weber, must at least account for the 'subjective intent' of practitioners. See Kronman, 1983, pp 22–28.

understand a practice one must employ the concepts, and the modes of understanding, of its practitioners. The opinion championed by Winch is fairly representative of ideas current in hermeneutic circles, and is also very similar to some of Dworkin's ideas. This small detour should serve to highlight some of Dworkin's affiliations with that intellectual movement.[30]

Winch's fourth chapter begins with an attack on the claim made by Vilfredo Pareto that the self-understanding of people engaged in a practice may be irrelevant to the true understanding of that practice. Pareto advances two principal claims in the excerpts quoted by Winch. The first states that the reasons people advance for their actions may fail to constitute adequate grounds for committing them: 'In the eyes of the Greek mariner', says Pareto, 'sacrifices to Poseidon and rowing with oars were equally logical means of navigation.'[31] However, that need not mean that things are in fact so: Greek mariners may have carried out their sacrifices for the purpose of guaranteeing a navigable sea, but a better understanding of their actions might insist, for example, that their actions were aimed at reducing anxiety in the face of unruly nature (through appeals to a powerful father-like figure). Indeed, given that these Greek mariners were totally wrong about the purposes that could be served by their actions, isn't it safe to assume that the correct understanding of their actions must be different than theirs?

Pareto's second claim is that some human practices remain the same from one culture or historical epoch to another, while their practitioners explain them in starkly different terms. It is then conceivable that the correct explanation would capture some deeper, more fundamental truth about these practices while discounting the self-understanding of their practitioners. Pareto adduces the case of baptism, which Christianity explains as the purification of the original sin. Baptism is a practice common to many cultures that do not possess the idea of an original sin. It is then at least a possibility that baptism can be better explained in terms different from those used by its Christian practitioners. Here is another example: in *History of Sexuality* Michel Foucault surveys the various justifications offered through the ages for the practice of sexual monogamy.[32] That practice was seen by its practitioners as serving the purpose of individual self-possession (associated with the Classical Greek ideal of moderation), of religious piety (the Catholic doctrine tolerating sex only within the confines of the institution of marriage), and of faithfulness to a loved one (the modern understanding of romantic love and 'betrayal'). It is at least conceivable that the most accurate way to understand

---

30 That is the hermeneutic tradition of Dilthey and his more or less faithful followers (like Gadamer and Habermas, whom Dworkin mentions), with their insistence on the indispensability of adopting the 'internal' perspective in the understanding of social phenomena.

31 Pareto, 1935, p 23.

32 Foucault, 1979.

the practice and its requirements is to look beyond practitioners' own proclamations about it.[33]

Now Winch opposes Pareto's two claims with the same criticism:

Two things may be called 'the same' or 'different' only with reference to a set of criteria which lay down what is to be regarded as a relevant difference. When the 'things' in question are purely physical the criteria appealed to will of course be that of the observer. But when one is dealing with intellectual (or indeed any kind of social) 'things', that is not so. For their *being* intellectual or social, as opposed to physical, in character depends entirely on their belonging in a certain way to a system of ideas or mode of living. It is only by reference to the criteria governing that system of ideas or mode of life that they have any existence as intellectual or social events. It follows that if the sociological investigator wants to regard them *as* social events (as, *ex hypothesi*, he must), he has to take seriously the criteria which are applied for distinguishing 'different' kinds of action and identifying the 'same' kinds of action within the way of life he is studying. It is not open to him arbitrarily to impose his own standards from without. In so far as he does so, the events he is studying lose altogether their character as *social* events. A Christian would strenuously deny that the baptism rites of his faith were really the same in character as the acts of a pagan ...[34]

According to Winch it is a mistake to try to understand such practices by employing an understanding that is independent of the practitioner's understanding. The correct understanding of Greek mariners' sacrifices must involve itself in the 'way of life' of the mariners: it must look at things, as Winch puts it, 'from the inside'. Attempting to understand the practice in terms alien to the practitioners – as some failed attempt to exercise control over the environment, for example – is of necessity to misunderstand its true meaning. That practice consists in worshipping a god – with all that this entails – and not in some failed engineering effort. Again, to properly understand the practice of monogamy one must employ the modes of understanding of its practitioners; to understand that practice in external terms is simply to misunderstand it *as a social practice*.

These claims have great similarity to many of the claims made by Dworkin.[35] Like Winch, Dworkin believes that a true understanding of a social practice requires the interpreter to look at the practice 'from within': to stand, as it were, side by side with its practitioners. He says that: 'A social scientist who offers to interpret the practice [of courtesy] must ... use the methods his

---

33 Claude Lévi-Strauss, coming from a somewhat different perspective, puts things this way: 'We know that among the most primitive peoples it is very difficult to obtain a moral justification or a rational explanation for any custom or institution. When he is questioned, the native merely answers that things have always been this way, that such was the command of the gods or the teaching of the ancestors. Even when interpretations are offered, they always have the character of rationalisations or secondary elaborations. There is rarely any doubt that the unconscious reasons for practising custom or sharing a belief are remote from the reasons given to justify them.' Lévi-Strauss, 1968, p 18.

34 Winch, 1990, p 108.

35 Also to some famous claims made by Wittgenstein (who is, in fact, the principal hero of Winch's book) – to which both Dworkin and Winch appeal.

subjects use in forming their own opinions about what courtesy really requires. He must, that is, *join* the practice he proposes to understand.'[36] That means, among other things, employing the conceptual apparatus of the practitioners, and sharing in their 'form of life' – in short, offering an understanding that employs the practice's own internal criteria.[37] Like Winch, Dworkin is also waging a war against positivists who purport to interpret social practices by merely 'observing' them and then speaking the language of 'facts'.

Now there is a level at which Winch's claims are indisputable: can one really understand a magical rite when viewing it as failed science? Can we really understand the Christian practice of baptism while ignoring the idea of the original sin? Would we be understanding monogamy if we viewed it not as a requirement of romantic fidelity but as a practice aimed at preserving the nuclear family unit? There is no doubt a *sense* that is lost in an interpretation not employing practitioners' own understanding. Winch wants to conclude from this that the *only* true way to try to understand a practice is through the self-understanding of its practitioners.[38] This claim is patently wrong: there are different methods and concepts (other than practitioners' own) through which we may seek to understand social practices 'as social phenomena'. Still, we must examine whether the sort of understanding that Dworkin is talking about – an articulation of *the conditions making a claim legally correct or incorrect* – must be restricted to practitioners' own perspective. If so, this may help support the desirability requirement: perhaps Winch's claim – or the part of it that we feel obliged to accept – can lend some much needed support to Dworkin's 'best light'.[39]

---

36 Dworkin, 1986, p 64. See also 'A social scientist must participate in a social practice if he hopes to understand it …' (p 55).

37 Practitioners, says Dworkin: 'must agree about a great deal in order to share a social practice. They must share a vocabulary … They must understand the world in sufficiently similar ways and have interests and convictions sufficiently similar to recognise the sense in each other's claims [about the practice] … That means not just using the same dictionary but sharing what Wittgenstein called a form of life sufficiently concrete so that one can recognise sense and purpose in what the other says and does … They must all "speak the same language" in both senses of that phrase.' Dworkin, 1986, pp 63–74. The *interpreter* must presumably share all these as well.

38 'Magic, in a society in which it occurs, plays a peculiar role of its own and is conducted according to considerations of its own … To try to understand magic by reference to the aims and nature of scientific activity [that is, by reference to considerations different from those used by its practitioners], as Pareto does, will necessarily be to *mis*understand it.' Winch, 1990, p 100 (original emphasis).

39 In a similar vein, Jürgen Habermas says that legal realism is a critique which 'relies on an observer's point of view' and that consequently 'the realists cannot explain how the functionally necessary accomplishments of the legal system [which for Habermas include some notion of the certainty of legal determinations] are compatible with a radical scepticism on the part of legal experts'. Habermas, 1996, p 201. I find it a mystery in what way such accomplishments are 'necessary', and why the realists must 'reconcile' them with their radical scepticism.

But, alas, Winch's claim does not help.[40] Interpretations of social practices which fail to employ practitioners' own understanding (their own opinions and methods) also profess to describe what makes a move within the practice *correct* or *incorrect* (or, in the case of legal practice, what makes a claim legally valid). Take, for example, Freud's interpretation of the frequently recurring tribal taboo barring the mother of a married woman from the presence of her son-in-law. According to Freud, the taboo seeks to thwart the sexual attraction the mother is bound to feel towards her son-in-law (and he goes on to explain the sources of this sexual appeal).[41] This interpretation is very different, of course, from the understandings offered by the practice's own practitioners (indeed one can only imagine these practitioners' horrified protestations); but it certainly purports to say – just as practitioners' own understanding does – why a certain conduct is a violation of the taboo while other conduct is not. Similarly, the economic analysis of law is very different from the understanding (the opinions and methods) of the judges whose determinations it seeks to explain (maximising economic efficiency is certainly not what these judges thought they were doing); and yet it does purport to articulate the conditions making a claim legally valid. The insistence on practitioners' own perspective becomes even more doubtful given that legal practitioners *themselves* accept the law and economics interpretation as sound, despite its variation from the self-understanding of previous practitioners.

On the other hand, if the law and economics interpretation of tort law, or Freud's interpretation of tribal taboos, *do* somehow count as 'internal' perspectives (the claim being that judicial determinations sought to maximise economic efficiency *whether the judges were aware of this or not*), then Winch's claims do not help either: if the 'internal' perspective may encompass unconscious and unarticulated conceptions, then there seems to be no basis for the claim that the 'internal' perspective must be desirable (for this is a claim which appears to be grounded in practitioners' *conscious* understanding alone).

Practitioners' mistake

There is another rather obvious point. Even if we could somehow defend the idea that the true conception of legal practice must agree with practitioners' self-understanding, still we would not end up with the desirability requirement – because practitioners may simply be wrong about what is desirable. Dworkin asserts not only that a true understanding of legal practice must portray legal practice as the most desirable *in the eyes of practitioners*; he insists that a true understanding must portray legal practice as *desirable in fact*. However, there surely remains the possibility that practitioners believe a conception of law to be highly desirable whereas in fact it is highly undesirable. Practitioners may think that following linguistic conventions in

---

40 It does not help even if we put aside the possibility of practitioners' bad faith, which this suggestion fails in any case to handle.

41 Freud, 1960.

the application of legal rules is a desirable conception of law because they think it produces predictable and easily ascertainable legal requirements. But this may prove to be a misguided illusion: perhaps legal interpretation guided by such linguistic conventions may be shown to produce highly unpredictable and uncertain legal requirements. Practitioners may believe they are practising according to a most desirable conception of law, but they may be wrong: history is littered with practices taken to be desirable and then discredited as downright pernicious. Again, if practitioners can be wrong about the desirability of a conception of law, then desirability cannot even be a criterion for practitioners' own understanding of the true conception (let alone a criterion for the true conception itself).

IV   The error and the insight

The error

To sum up, the problem with deriving the desirability requirement from practitioners' own understanding concerns the possible gap between practitioners' own understanding and the determinative conception of law, as well as the possibility of error in assessing desirability. Now in fact Dworkin agrees that the true conception of law need not accord with practitioners' own understanding: indeed he commits himself to this position by rejecting the idea that the true conception of law is the one shared among legal practitioners (there is, he says, no such shared understanding). This means that the 'truth' of a conception cannot be a function of its agreement with practitioners' own understanding but a function of its own theoretical merit – and it therefore also means that the true conception does not accord with many practitioners' understanding of it. Indeed Dworkin explicitly says that: 'an interpretation need not be consistent ... with how past judges saw what they were doing, in order to count as an eligible interpretation of what they in fact did ... [W]e cannot reject [an] interpretation on the sole ground that it would have amazed the judges whose decisions it proposes to interpret.'[42] But once we insert a

---

42 Dworkin, 1986, p 285. There is no necessary contradiction between the claim that the correct conception of legal practice must accord with practitioners' own understanding and the claim that the best conception of legal practice may surprise legal practitioners. What it means for a conception to 'accord' with an understanding may very well be a flexible thing, and practitioners may be surprised by a conception which, upon a deeper reflection, they may recognise (as Dworkin also notes) as a truer understanding of their practice than the one they themselves hold. A lexicographer may spend her life writing dictionaries while believing – and indeed carrying on her work trying to execute this belief as best she can – that her endeavour consists in the mere enunciation of the conventional understanding of terms. Yet philosophers of language may reject this belief as a misleading oversimplification: the work of lexicographers consists not in the mere enunciation of conventional understandings but in the articulation of the essential, that is to say the important, features of terms – at times in *opposition* to what most people take them to be. Now this articulation of the lexicographer's practice may appear to our lexicographer, on first sight, as surprising; but she may come to recognise this latter view as superior to her own.

wedge between practitioners' own understanding of the practice and its true conception, what can be the justification for the claim that desirability is a criterion for a true conception of law? What can justify an acknowledgment that the true conception might have 'amazed' the practitioners whose decisions it proposes to interpret while insisting that that conception must be desirable? It is impossible to defend the best light requirement by relying on practitioners' own understanding of their practice; but where else can it come from? Dworkin has been recently occupying himself with this question – though so far (it seems to me) with little success.[43] And the more one considers the problem, the less likely it seems that Dworkin can pull this rabbit out of his hat.

The conclusion of all this is that the best light requirement – unlike the requirement of fit – is not a criterion for the true conception of law. The latter requirement is indeed necessary; we cannot be offering a good interpretation of legal practice if our interpretation leaves out much of that practice. If we fail along the dimension of fit, our conception is by this fact alone untrue. The fit requirement is, in fact, a methodological triviality: it merely means that a theory that fails to explain much of the data it is supposed to be a theory *of*, must be wrong. But the requirement of best light is a different matter altogether: it appears to derive from practitioners' own understanding of their practice, and it therefore can be proved wrong just as practitioners' own understanding can. The best light may be a necessary requirement for the judicial discourse; but that discourse need not be determinative, nor need it be *in fact* desirable.

In *Law's Empire* Dworkin dedicates long pages to demonstrating that the economic conception of law is less desirable than alternative conceptions of law;[44] and that legal positivism is undesirable because it does not sit well with democratic theory.[45] Such discussions play an important role in jurisprudential debates: the fact that law and economics or legal positivism are undesirable conceptions of law may have an impact on what legal practitioners actually do, or on scholarly attempts to influence what they do. But these arguments do not prove what Dworkin believes they prove: legal positivism may not sit well with democratic theory; but what of it? This tells us little on whether legal positivism is a correct understanding of law. It is perfectly true that legal scholars often combine the quest for a true conception of law with the quest for a conception of law putting legal practice in its best light. To be sure, the wish to justify a social practice is frequently the very purpose of articulating an interpretation of it. (Dworkin is right when he claims that legal positivism, despite its protestation to the contrary, is such a theory of law.) But Dworkin is wrong in claiming that there is no distinction to be had between these two efforts. An interpretation may claim to be the most desirable conception of law without also claiming to be a true conception. It may say: this understanding of legal practice is not an understanding of how legal practice really works; it

---

43 Dworkin, 2000.

44 See Dworkin, 1986, pp 277–312.

45 See Dworkin, 1986, pp 139–50.

is an understanding of how legal practice should work, because that would be a wonderful thing. But it is still an understanding of our legal practice because it is a claim about the logical possibilities of our practice: about what it is good for legal practice to be and about what it can be, though not necessarily about what it is. And conversely, an interpretation may obviously claim to be a true conception of law without being the most desirable.

This point can be easily demonstrated through the case of *critical* legal theories, which Dworkin (erroneously) believes must compete along the dimension of desirability. Critical legal theories need do nothing of the kind. This is obvious if only from the fact that a critical legal theory may seek to *redescribe* a supposedly desirable conception. For example, practitioners may think that law and economics presents a desirable conception of private law; but it is conceivable that legal determinations guided by the maximisation of economic efficiency are consistently biased in favour of the wealthy and to the detriment of the poor: maybe our existing economic arrangements are such that the maximisation of efficiency – so it happens – tends to benefit the rich at the expense of the disadvantaged. Now if such were the case with the economic analysis of law, then law and economics' proposed conditions of legal validity could be captured from a presumably undesirable perspective: legal validity would be a function of a legal right's tendency to perpetuate existing (and potentially unjust) distribution of resources. There is no reason to think that one description of this legal conception would be *truer* than the other: the maximisation of economic efficiency and the enriching of the rich may amount to the very same thing. Obviously, the possibility of a critical redescription cuts against the idea that the truth of a conception of law is a function of its desirability.

But Dworkin may have a different claim in mind: not that the redescription is necessarily *untrue*, but that it is untrue *as a conception of law*. In other words, it may be true that the law and economics conception of law is biased against the poor; but even if things are so (the claim goes), this is not an *essential* part of law and economics: we can easily imagine the maximisation of efficiency as *not* being biased against the poor. A theory of a social practice is aimed at capturing the practice's *essence* (what the practice is *about*), not its contingencies. The institution of marriage may bring an increase in the sales of diamonds; but marriage is not about increasing diamond sales: that would be an untrue theory of marriage.

There are two responses to this claim. First, that an undesirable consequence is not what the practice is *about* is precisely what many critical conceptions dispute: the bias against the poor, the Marxists would say, *is* the essence of legal practice. If law and economics were not biased against the poor, then law and economics would not have been the criteria of legal validity. Broadly speaking, the *essential* features of legal practice need not be desirable. But there is an even simpler response to the above claim: if this is what Dworkin means by his best light requirement, then Dworkin's claim is insignificant. Suppose that the critic offering the undesirable redescription of law and economics concedes Dworkin's point: bias against the poor, she says, is indeed not an *essential* feature of legal practice (we can easily imagine legal practice which is not biased against the poor). Now what on earth is the significance of that concession? It seems to have none. If this is what the best light requirement is about, then it is an uninteresting thesis. And yet there is much insight in Dworkin's claims.

The insight

I have discussed the accuracy of Dworkin's claim that legal practitioners consider the desirability of the arguments underlying legal claims as important for their legal validity. I now wish to examine the relations between this important observation and some other aspects of Dworkin's legal theory.

As we saw, Dworkin begins his attack on legal positivism by noting that legal practitioners habitually disagree about the correct legal rights and duties, and about what makes them correct. Now the commonness of such disagreements is undeniable (they exist in every case arriving before a court, for example); but legal positivism has downplayed the implications of this phenomenon for the understanding of law. HLA Hart, as we saw, claimed that such disagreements exist only on the 'margins of [legal] rules': it is only where the law 'runs out' that such genuine disagreements arise.[46] Hart's point is an upshot of the positivist claim that the correct legal requirements are a matter of (non-controversial) conventional agreement – conventions about where to look for authoritative legal rules, and then linguistic and interpretive conventions in applying those rules. Only when these conventions fail to point to one resolution in a given case (when the language of the identified rule is ambiguous under the circumstances, for example) do genuine legal disagreements arise. (Legal practitioners may of course disagree all the time, but many of these disagreements are disingenuous – as when lawyers proclaim the legal requirements which suit their clients rather than those they ought to know the law actually requires.) It follows that genuine disagreements are not about what the law *is*, for what it *is* must be a matter of conventional agreement (indeed the law is what it is by virtue of this conventional agreement); instead, these are disputes about what the law *should be*: genuine disagreements arise precisely where the law is no longer around. In fact, looked at from this peculiar perspective, the more genuine disagreements we have regarding a particular legal issue, the less law we have regarding it. Such disagreements are, for the most part, disagreements about issues 'external to the law' – moral issues or economic issues or political issues or what have you – and the arguments they involve are similar to the arguments of legislators deliberating over proposed legislation.[47] Such

---

46 See Hart, 1994, p 135.

47 According to Joseph Raz, certain legal disagreements may in fact be about the law: these are disagreements about what the ruling convention is. See Raz, 1998, for advancing this argument. Still, once a convention is the subject of dispute, it is doubtful that it is still a convention in any respect that is significant here.

arguments, say the positivists, are often advanced as claims about what the law is; but they are best understood as claims about what the law should be: if you take a good look at these arguments you see that they are not the mere descriptions of the state of the law that they purport to be, but that instead they appeal, whether implicitly or (often enough) explicitly, to what is *desirable* about the right or duty that they proclaim.

Dworkin turns all this around: he argues that these pervasive disagreements are legal disputes *par excellence* – that they are (as they claim to be) disagreements about what the law *is*, not about what it should be. Dworkin transforms what for the positivists is an unfortunate though, perhaps, inevitable *modus operandi* – the dirty little secret of legal practice which Austin has branded a 'childish fiction'[48] (that is, practitioners purporting to say what the law *is* while making normative claims about what the law should be) – into a fundamental aspect of legal argumentation and legal decision-making. There is nothing childish about purporting to ascertain what the law is while making normative claims: this is precisely what ascertaining the law is about! If the positivists see this as an institutional deception, it is only because their understanding of law is too simple.

Dworkin proceeds to elaborate this claim with his 'interpretive attitude' – the idea that practitioners establish the correct legal rights and duties by seeking those which derive from the most desirable conception of law. This hypothesis explains the commonness of legal disagreements: practitioners habitually disagree about what the law is because they disagree about which conception is the most desirable (desirability obviously being a controversial matter). It also accounts for the normative element in legal claims – for the way in which a claim's desirability supports its legal validity: it is the desirability of the *theoretical conception from which a claim derives* (rather than the desirability of the claim itself) which infuses legal discourse with normativity. Dworkin channels this normative element into a respectable outlet: the positivists explained this normative element away by insisting it is not really about the law; Dworkin insists that it is about the law, but that it is a perfectly respectable lady. (The lady's reputation is then further enhanced by the claim that there is *one* correct most desirable conception of law.[49])

Now I think that there is much that is wrong in the hypothesis of the 'interpretive attitude' (I do not think, for example, that the normative element of

---

48 '[T]he childish fiction employed by our judges, that judiciary or common law is not made by them, but is a miraculous something made by nobody, existing, I suppose, from eternity, and merely declared from time to time by judges.' Austin, 1879, p 655. Austin speaks against the claim, which he sees implicit in judges' pronouncements, that establishing legal rights and duties is never a matter of 'personal' judgment differing from one judge to another. Since things are obviously not so, and judges do often issue judgments whose content would have been different if decided by a different judge, Austin concludes that in such cases they do not really declare the law (as they claim they do) but in fact write it. Implicit in his claim is the assumption that legal rights and duties cannot be controversial.

49 That claim is put forward, among other places, in Dworkin, 1996.

legal arguments consists in the desirability of their underlying 'conception of law'), but Dworkin has touched upon an important point in insisting that determining what the law *is* is a process involving claims for desirability – for goodness. His theory joins a number of efforts seeking to explain the role of desirability in determinations of legal validity (and thereby to substitute the seemingly irremediable account of natural law).[50] So Dworkin's methodological claims are wrong; but his attempt to explain the normative nature of legal discourse as an *essential* aspect of establishing the content of the law (and not an unfortunate if unavoidable game that practitioners play) pulls legal philosophy in the right direction: legal discourse is infused with claims about what *ought* to be done because what the law *is* is, *in some way*, what ought to be done.

To conclude: we saw Dworkin's methodological claims, and the way Dworkin sought to defend the impartiality of his methodological process; and we also saw that these claims failed – despite the fact that they struck in the right direction. But the failure of Dworkin's methodological claims need not mean that his *substantive* suggestion (his own conception of law) also fails; so I will now move to examine the merit of Dworkin's conception of law, which he calls 'law as integrity'. As we shall soon see, many of the claims advanced by 'law as integrity' would be made clear by our theme: the idea that establishing the impartiality of legal interpretation is a principal project for modern legal theorists.

---

50 See, eg, Hart and Sacks, 2001; Frankfurter, 1947. The most important legal theorist to propound such a view was Lon Fuller (despite Fuller's own unfortunate identification of his theory with natural law): see Fuller, 1969.

I Dworkin's thesis

Following his exposition of the methodological claims of fit and best light, Dworkin moves to propose his own conception of law – the theory *he* believes best fits legal practice and puts it in its best light. This theory – 'law as integrity' – describes legal interpretation essentially as follows: the legal interpreter first arrives at a set of *moral principles* that fit the 'institutional legal materials' and put them in their best light; and then, using those principles, the interpreter establishes the correct legal rights and duties. Thus (confusingly enough for the reader, though perhaps unsurprisingly), Dworkin's conception of law reintroduces the fit and best light requirements as criteria for the correct set of moral principles from which all legal determinations derive. Section I explains Dworkin's theory and examines its merit (concluding that it presents an unintelligible description of what 'integrity' is), while section II addresses the relation between 'law as integrity' and the impartiality of legal interpretation. As we shall see, according to 'law as integrity' *proper* legal interpretation is always impartial.

'Law as integrity': presentation

As previously discussed, Dworkin maintains that a theory of legal practice must hypothesise a function or a purpose (however vague or abstract) that is served by the law.[1] Now according to Dworkin's own theory, the purpose of the law is the *justification of state coercion*: the law is aimed at justifying the way in which the state exercises its coercive powers. The law fulfils this purpose, says Dworkin, by demanding that every legal requirement conform to certain moral principles. What moral principles are these? These are the moral principles which best 'fit and justify' the 'institutional legal materials'. The 'institutional legal materials' are all the statutes and precedents and regulations of administrative agencies and other such materials from official legal sources. The legal interpreter, examining these legal materials, must arrive at a set of moral principles that best fits these materials and puts them in their best light. For example, the principle that a man may not benefit from a wrong he committed is presumably a principle that fits the legal materials (it underlies many statutes and many judicial doctrines), and it puts these materials in their best light (it makes these materials look good and desirable). Any legal requirement must then conform, in some way (we will examine how), to this principle. So the method with which legal interpreters arrive at

---

1 See Chapter 4, section entitled 'The best theory: "fit" and "justification"'.

the correct legal rights and duties is essentially this: they first arrive at a set of moral principles which is evidenced in the institutional legal materials (that is, that fits the legal materials) and which makes these legal materials appear good and desirable (that is, that puts these materials in their best light); and they then proceed to determine what the law requires by making sure that any legal requirement conforms to these moral principles.

(One should not confuse the two tests employing the 'fit and best light' requirements: as we saw in the previous chapter, according to Dworkin the correct conception of law is the conception that best fits legal practice and puts it in its best light. This is one test. Now Dworkin believes that the correct conception of law is the conception he calls 'law as integrity', and according to that conception the correct legal requirements are those which conform to the set of moral principles that best fits the institutional legal materials and puts them in their best light. This is the *second* test. These two tests are independent of each other.)

So according to 'law as integrity' all legal requirements must conform to the set of moral principles that best fits legal practice and puts it in its best light. It is essential for Dworkin that all legal requirements conform to one and the same 'set of moral principles' or 'scheme of justice' (Dworkin uses these two expressions interchangeably, and so will I).[2] The law, says Dworkin, must 'speak with one voice': a proposition is legally valid only if it conforms to the same set of moral principles to which all other legal propositions conform. So long as all legal propositions are interrelated in this way, the law 'speaks with one voice', because any utterance it makes agrees with the set of moral principles with which all its other utterances agree.

Now what is meant by the idea of one 'set of moral principles' or one 'scheme of justice'? Dworkin elaborates on these notions in the following way:

> We know that [moral] principles we accept independently sometimes conflict in the sense that we cannot satisfy both on some particular occasion. We might believe, for example, that people should be free to do what they wish with their own property and also that people should begin life on equal terms. Then the question arises whether rich people should be permitted to leave their wealth to their children, and we might believe that our two principles pull in opposite directions on that issue. Our model demands ... that the resolution of this conflict itself be principled. A scheme of inheritance taxes might recognise both principles in a certain relation by setting rates of tax that are less than confiscatory. But we insist that whatever relative weighting of the two principles the solution assumes must flow throughout the scheme, and that other decisions, on other matters that involve the same two principles, respect that weighting as well.[3]

Thus 'integrity' – which is the name Dworkin gives to the demand that the law 'speak with one voice' – does not require that all our laws conform to a set of moral principles which never conflict among themselves in their practical

---

2 Dworkin, 1986, p 165.
3 Dworkin, 1986, pp 435–36 (fn 7).

counsels (this would be a rather absurd demand); instead, integrity demands that a certain chosen priority or ranking among moral principles be maintained – throughout the particular legal scheme, and throughout the legal system as a whole.

Dworkin's argument for 'law as integrity'

Dworkin argues for this understanding of law and its test of legal validity along the two dimensions he believes to constitute the criteria for the correct theory of law – fit and best light. (As we saw, the best light requirement is misconceived; but Dworkin's elaboration of the claim that 'law as integrity' puts legal practice in its best light will help us better understand – or try to understand – what Dworkin means by 'integrity'.) Dworkin's principal argument in defence of 'law as integrity' appeals to our instinct: our instinct demonstrates that we value the idea of integrity, and that we expect our laws to respect it – even if we have never given ourselves a conscious account of this. 'Law as integrity' is a conception that fits the legal materials, as an investigation would presumably show, because we already use integrity in shaping our law; and 'law as integrity' puts legal practice in its best light because, as Dworkin will argue, integrity is an important value of political morality – which is why we appreciate and respect it to begin with. In other words, Dworkin's theory purports to bring to light a hitherto unarticulated but existing understanding of law: 'Astronomers', says Dworkin, 'postulated Neptune before they discovered it. They knew that only another planet, whose orbit lay beyond those already recognised, could explain the behaviour of the nearer planets. Our instinct … suggests another political idea standing beside justice and fairness. Integrity is our Neptune'.[4]

What is the 'instinct' of which Dworkin speaks, and which occupies such an important place in the argument for integrity? That instinct, says Dworkin, manifests itself in our rejection of legal 'checkerboard solutions'. He writes:

> Do the people of North Dakota disagree whether justice requires compensation for product defects that manufacturers could not reasonably have prevented? Then why should their legislature not impose this 'strict' liability on manufacturers of automobiles but not on manufacturers of washing machines? Do the people of Alabama disagree about the morality of racial discrimination? Why should their legislature not forbid racial discrimination on buses but permit it in restaurants?[5]

The reason why we feel that it shouldn't, says Dworkin, lies with our respect for integrity: 'If there must be a compromise because people are divided about justice, then the compromise must be external, not internal; it must be a compromise about which scheme of justice to adopt rather than a compromised scheme of justice.'[6] The law must 'settle on some coherent

4   Dworkin, 1986, p 183.
5   Dworkin, 1986, p 178.
6   Dworkin, 1986, p 179.

principle' and never 'affirm for some people a principle it denies to others'.[7] An example of a law settling on a coherent principle, says Dworkin, is a statute prohibiting abortion which contains an exception for pregnancies caused by rape; an example of a law failing to settle on a coherent principle is a statute permitting abortion only to 'women born in one specified decade each century': only the former constitutes a 'principled' statutory scheme.[8]

Principled v unprincipled statutory schemes

Looking at Dworkin's abortion statutes, it seems that the crucial difference between the 'principled' statute and the checkerboard statute (which permits abortion only for women born in the 1950s) is that in the former, but not in the latter, we identify a justification for the different treatment the statute accords the two categories. The question to which we demand an answer – and which only the former statute can supply – is 'what is it in the class of cases that falls within and that which falls without the statute's directive that accounts for this distinction between them?'. It is presumably the absence of such a justification which makes the checkerboard statute unacceptable to us. This idea, as Dworkin also notes, is expressed in the notion of 'equality before the law': the similarly situated are to be treated similarly. Equality before the law appears to demand that the different treatment accorded different categories be justified by the difference between these categories. In short, we expect the distinctions our statutes make to be principled distinctions, and neither of the distinctions made by Dworkin's examples of checkerboard statutes is principled.

As we shall see, Dworkin sees things somewhat differently; but he does seem to recognise that the problem with checkerboard statutes is that they lack a reason for treating their classes differently: 'Shall we just say', he says, 'that a checkerboard solution is unjust by definition because it treats different people differently *for no good reason*, and justice requires treating like cases alike? This suggestion seems in the right neighbourhood ...'[9] What does Dworkin mean here by 'a good reason'? He says that so long as we can 'recognise' a reason for treating different people differently, a legal scheme is not a checkerboard solution – even if we think that reason weak or even plain wrong: 'Suppose you think abortion is murder and that it makes no difference whether the pregnancy is the result of rape. Would you not think a statute prohibiting abortion except in the case of rape distinctly better than a statute prohibiting abortion except for women born in one specified decade each century? ... You see the first of these statutes as a solution that gives effect to two recognisable principles of justice, ordered in a certain way, even though you reject one of the principles.'[10] The former statute is not a checkerboard statute (and is therefore 'distinctly better') because the exception it contains is grounded in a recognised

---

7 Dworkin, 1986, pp 179 and 183.

8 Dworkin, 1986, p 183.

9 Dworkin, 1986, pp 183–84.

10 Dworkin, 1986, p 183.

reason for treating different people differently (that reason being the woman's complete lack of responsibility for the pregnancy, and perhaps the misery awaiting the unwanted child) – even if that reason (or principle) is one we reject. In an appended footnote Dworkin adds: 'We can easily imagine other examples of compromises [that is, compromised statutes] we would accept as not being violations of integrity because they reflect principles of justice we recognise though we do not ourselves endorse them.'[11] It is enough that a statute's drawn distinctions are supported by principles we can recognise – even if not endorse – to make it a principled (rather than a checkerboard) statute. In short, in contradistinction to statutes whose distinctions are grounded in recognised principles, checkerboard statutes draw distinctions which are arbitrary: there are underlying principles for treating pregnancies caused by rape differently from other pregnancies in regulating abortion; but there seem to be no underlying principles for treating women born in one decade differently from women born in another.

Does integrity fit the legal materials?

Recall that 'integrity' demands that all legal requirements conform to one 'set of moral principles' or one 'scheme of justice'. Now given what underlies the distinction between checkerboard statutes and principled ones, between internal and external compromises, how do checkerboard statutes (and our instinct in regard to them) support the case for integrity? Dworkin's answer is surprisingly straightforward. What underwrites our aversion to checkerboard statutes, he says, is our respect for integrity: 'The most natural explanation of why we oppose checkerboard statutes appeals to [integrity]: we say that a state that adopts these internal compromises is acting in an unprincipled way … [I]t must endorse principles to justify part of what it has done that it must reject to justify the rest.'[12] Checkerboard statutes, in other words, do not conform to one scheme of justice: we expect our law to 'speak with one voice' (that is, to follow from the same set of principles throughout), and in checkerboard statutes we hear the sounds of various voices.

But far from being 'natural', this explanation is quite baffling: there is a sea of difference between the expectation that statutes draw distinctions which conform to some recognised principle (which is what is lacking in checkerboard statutes), and the expectation that statutes draw distinctions which conform to the very same set of principles to which all other legal rights and duties conform. Obviously, a statutory distinction may conform to a recognised principle which does not belong to the set of principles to which all other legal requirements conform. In that case that statute would not be a checkerboard statute; but it would certainly violate integrity (for, to repeat, integrity demands not only that legal requirements be supported by recognised principles, but that those principles be equally in force throughout

---

11 Dworkin, 1986, p 436 (fn 8).
12 Dworkin, 1986, pp 183–84.

the legal system). In fact, Dworkin's very examples of 'principled' statutes – those statutes which do *not* offend our checkerboard instincts – may very well fail to respect integrity. It is true, of course, that the presence of a recognised principle is a *prerequisite* for the very possibility of Dworkin's integrity: if laws habitually exhibited the unprincipled distinctions we see in checkerboard statutes, integrity could not have even been a possibility. There can be no unprincipled statutory scheme which respects integrity. But there can be principled statutory schemes which do not. So our checkerboard instincts fall far short of endorsing integrity's holism: they can be appeased where integrity is lacking, and it therefore cannot be the case that what gives rise to our aversion to checkerboard statutes is our aspiration for integrity.

So in fact we are dealing here with two independent notions (on the one hand the idea that treating seemingly similar people differently need be justified by a recognised principle, on the other – integrity, the idea that treating seemingly similar people differently need be justified by the set of principles justifying all other legal rights and duties), and no quick inference can be made from the respect for the one notion to the respect for the other. Yet Dworkin collapses these two notions, simply believing them to be one (thinking that the lack of integrity is simply the problem with checkerboard *broadly applied*: lack of integrity is arbitrariness generalised from the case of specific statutory schemes to the law as a whole, and the aversion for checkerboard solutions is but a particular case of the general impulse for integrity).[13] This, however, appears to be a mistake.

Dworkin repeatedly attempts to explain the problem with checkerboard statutes by appealing to the ideal of integrity: he claims, for example, that with checkerboard statutes: 'one principle of justice is not outweighed or qualified by another in some way that expresses a ranking of the two. Only a single principle is involved; it is affirmed for one group and denied for another, and this is what our sense of propriety denounces.'[14] (Lack of integrity is, presumably, precisely the manifestation of this latter problem: that a certain principle, or a set of principles, is denied in one case and affirmed in another.) But this identification of the two problems does not work (the two, as I said, are distinct). The distinction between checkerboard statutes and principled ones cannot be a distinction between legal schemes which 'affirm' a principle to one group and deny it to another, and legal schemes that do not: both checkerboard statutes and principled ones 'affirm a principle for one group and deny it to another'. For instance, in the rape exception abortion statute (Dworkin's example of a principled statute) the principle to which the rape

---

13 Dworkin says that 'checkerboard statutes are the most dramatic violations of the ideal of integrity', yet 'integrity is flouted not only in *specific* compromises of that character ... but whenever a community enacts and enforces different laws each of which is coherent in itself, but which cannot be defended together as expressing a coherent ranking of different principles of justice or fairness or procedural due process'. Dworkin, 1986, p 184 (emphasis added).

14 Dworkin, 1986, p 436 (fn 7).

exception conforms (presumably, the principle of individual autonomy) is affirmed for one group of women (those whose pregnancies are caused by rape) and denied to all others. To claim that the checkerboard/non-checkerboard distinction revolves around whether a statute 'expresses a ranking of conflicting principles' or 'affirms conflicting ones' is merely to play with words.

Here is another unsuccessful attempt to explain the problem with checkerboard statutes in terms of integrity. Principled statutes, says Dworkin, present the same ranking of principles throughout: 'A scheme of inheritance taxes might recognise [two conflicting] principles in a certain relation by setting rates of tax that are less than confiscatory. But we insist that whatever relative weighting of the two principles the solution assumes must *flow throughout the scheme* ...'[15] This, once more, is precisely what integrity demands. Presumably, our checkerboard instincts are not offended by the scheme of inheritance taxes – despite the fact that it conforms to conflicting principles – because it manifests the same ranking of principles from beginning to end. Yet, the notion of a 'ranked set of principles' is always defined, by Dworkin, by reference to the legal scheme as a whole: the 'ranked set of principles' in the principled abortion statute which exempts rape-caused pregnancies includes the principles prohibiting abortion as well as the principles sanctioning them; and similarly here – the 'ranked set of principles' is given by the entire scheme of inheritance taxes. Consequently, it appears to be a logical impossibility to observe a legal scheme which does not manifest a consistent application of a set of principles throughout: the set of principles manifested in any legal scheme is necessarily the set constituted by that legal scheme in its entirety. The distinction between checkerboard and non-checkerboard statutes simply cannot be a distinction between a legal scheme which manifests the same ranking of principles from beginning to end and a legal scheme which does not. Indeed the example of a legal scheme which ranks conflicting principles but still violates integrity by failing to respect that ranking 'throughout' is one we badly need to see, but never get to.

There are more examples, but they are all symptoms of the same unhappy condition: Dworkin merges two independent ideas – the lack of a recognisable reason, or principle, for a drawn distinction (the checkerboard idea), and the lack of a recognisable reason, or principle, that is equally applicable all over the place (integrity). And even though there is *some* affinity between the two notions, it is certainly not the identity that Dworkin purports to see. Why does Dworkin think the two are identical? I think Dworkin believes that some notion of rationality underlies both the aversion towards unprincipled distinctions and the respect for integrity. As we saw, the problem with checkerboard statutes is ultimately their inability to justify the distinctions they draw between categories: they simply draw arbitrary distinctions. Now I think that Dworkin thinks – though he does not say so, nor does he attempt to

---

15 Dworkin, 1986, p 436 (fn 7) (emphasis added).

defend this position – that the problem with the lack of integrity is that it, too, must ultimately evidence arbitrariness: just as checkerboard statutes are arbitrary because they cannot justify treating one class in one way and another in another, so is it arbitrary to act according to one 'moral scheme' (or a 'set of principles') on one occasion and a different 'moral scheme' on another.[16]

The obvious problem with this hypothesis (which merges the arbitrariness of checkerboard statutes with the alleged arbitrariness of a lack of integrity) is that unlike the arbitrariness evidenced in checkerboard statutes, which we perceive as morally unacceptable, the kind of arbitrariness the lack of integrity is supposed to manifest is both morally acceptable and widely practised.[17] Thus if we take the notion of a 'moral scheme' to mean something like a moral theory or moral principles, there seems to be nothing unreasonable nor uncommon about justifying different moral positions by relying, on different occasions, upon different and potentially incompatible 'moral schemes': for example, there is nothing wrong with justifying one moral position by relying upon a strict utilitarian calculation ('this is justified because it creates the greatest benefit to the greatest number'), while justifying another by relying upon a theory of rights ('this is justified because it protects minorities from the tyranny of the majority') even if these two theories appear deeply irreconcilable. (And our statutes, of course, also derive from such eclectic justifications.)

Now as we shall soon see, Dworkin handles this difficulty by weakening the notion of a 'set of moral principles'. (If he didn't, he would have had to claim that some pretty sensible moral or statutory positions were morally unacceptable.) The result of this, I believe, is devastating for his theory, for it makes the notion of integrity utterly unintelligible. But this will become apparent later. For now it is sufficient to note that the arbitrariness of checkerboard statutes and the arbitrariness of the lack of integrity are independent of each other, even though, as I noted above, there is some affinity between the two: the absence of checkerboard statutes is a precondition for the existence of integrity, so that Dworkin's mistaken inference from one to the other is not a *perspicuous* error – though it is certainly an error. This is why Dworkin's inference may pass us by without causing a stir; but stir we should! That inference is unfounded: it draws unworkable distinctions, it sees identity where there is none to be found, and it leads us unsupported over a theoretical chasm that is in great need of justification, and that is possibly unbridgeable: we may all share an aversion for checkerboard statutes, but we may all reject the ideal of integrity with an equal distaste.

---

16 It is something akin to this hypothesis which recently brought Dworkin to pronounce his belief in the idea that our political, moral, and ethical values may all be mutually reconciled in a grand theoretical edifice. See Dworkin, 2000.

17 Another problem with this presumed identity is that Dworkin seems to assume (and for no good reason) that the arbitrariness of checkerboard statutes is strictly moral arbitrariness. I will not get into this issue here, but the following chapter will make it amply clear that the problem with checkerboard statutes is not necessarily moral at all.

(Indeed I think that our instincts, as well as a reasoned reflection, will utterly dispose of any intelligible notion of integrity as a political, moral, or legal ideal.[18]) To sum up, Dworkin's only argument for the fit of 'law as integrity' in fact offers that theory no support: the absence of checkerboard statutes tells us nothing about whether integrity 'fits' our laws. If integrity is our Neptune, we have yet to find its orbital indications.[19]

Is integrity desirable?

Now that the idea of integrity is detached from the bogus support of our checkerboard instinct, we must ask ourselves what makes integrity a desirable conception of law. According to Dworkin, integrity (which mandates that all laws conform to a 'single coherent scheme of principles'[20]) enhances the legitimacy of the state: 'I shall argue that a political society that accepts integrity as a political virtue thereby becomes a special form of a community, special in a way that promotes its moral authority to assume and deploy a monopoly of coercive force.'[21] This – he adds – is not the only desirable aspect of integrity:

> [Integrity also] provides protection against partiality or deceit or other forms of official corruption, for example. There is more room for favoritism or vindictiveness in a system that permits manufacturers of automobiles and of washing machines to be governed by different and contradictory principles of liability. Integrity also contributes to the efficiency of law … If people accept that they are governed not only by explicit rules laid down by past political decisions but by whatever other standards flow from the principles these decisions assume, then the set of recognised public standards can expand and contract organically, without the need for detailed legislation or adjudication on each possible point of conflict.[22]

In examining these allegedly desirable aspects of 'law as integrity' I will start with the lesser claims first. Integrity, says Dworkin, allows the set of recognised public standards to expand or contract beyond the rules laid down by past political decisions, thereby allowing us to forgo detailed legislation and adjudication on specific points. That under 'law as integrity' the set of legal standards expands or contracts 'beyond' these rules is obviously true, for

---

18 Interestingly enough, the fact that Dworkin's leap over this intellectual chasm has gone largely unnoticed may be partly attributed to the 'checkerboard' metaphor, which – as it turns out – has little to do with what is in fact wrong with these statutes and a lot to do with the idea of integrity.

19 The argument of checkerboard statutes is the only one Dworkin adduces for the claim that integrity fits the legal materials. Following his discussion of checkerboard statutes Dworkin writes: 'I shall offer no further argument for my claim that our political life recognises integrity as a political virtue. The case is now strong enough for the weight of interest to shift to the other dimension of interpretation [ie, desirability].' Dworkin, 1986, p 186.

20 Dworkin, 1986, p 214.

21 Dworkin, 1986, p 189.

22 Dworkin, 1986, p 188.

integrity sees no identity between legal standards and these rules (the rules must undergo the process of interpretation guided by the ideal of integrity before they yield the real legal standards). But the advantage of forgoing detailed legislation and adjudication can exist only where people agree about what integrity requires: if people disagree about what integrity requires on a given point then detailed legislation or adjudication will be needed in order to settle that issue. It is simply wrong to say, as Dworkin does, that 'This process works less effectively, to be sure, when people disagree, as inevitably they sometimes will, about which principles are in fact assumed by the explicit rules' – and hence about what integrity requires: if people disagree about what integrity requires then the process is not 'less effective' but not effective at all.[23] Hence in order to enjoy the advantage Dworkin proclaims, people must not only agree here and there – they must agree to a degree that expands (rather than contracts) the recognised public standards, otherwise we risk an *increase* in the need for detailed legislation and adjudication. But then, given what we know about integrity-based interpretations (as well as Dworkin's repetitive admissions as to their controversiality), it seems that integrity would be highly undesirable as far as the need for detailed adjudication and legislation is concerned.

Dworkin's second point in favour of integrity's desirability is that it protects against partiality or deceit or official corruption: 'There is more room for favoritism or vindictiveness in a system that permits manufacturers of automobiles and of washing machines to be governed by different and contradictory principles of liability.'[24] Now this advantage derives from the prohibition against checkerboard statutes; but integrity, as we saw, demands much more: it demands that each legal requirement be justified by a set of principles which justifies all other laws as well. As we saw, to satisfy integrity we may first have to enforce the prohibition against checkerboard statutes; but even so, the above argument tells us nothing about why integrity is desirable, only why the prohibition against checkerboard statutes is: if we can have such protection from official corruption without having integrity, then protection from official corruption is not one of integrity's desirable attributes.

So we arrive at Dworkin's principal argument for the desirability of integrity: that it enhances the legitimacy of the state. How so? Dworkin's argument is extremely obscure. He begins by looking to associative obligations – like those between members of a family or friends – to explain the legitimacy of the state (that is, 'its citizens' general obligation to obey the law').[25] These obligations, he says, are reciprocal in a way that embodies the following four characteristics: (1) they are 'special' – they hold only within the group; (2) they are personal – they run from person to person, not just towards the group as a

---

23 Dworkin, 1986, pp 188–89.

24 Dworkin, 1986, p 188.

25 'A state is legitimate if its constitutional structure and practices are such that its citizens have a general obligation to obey political decisions that purport to impose duties on them.' Dworkin, 1986, p 191.

whole; (3) they evidence real concern for the welfare of others; and (4) they not only presuppose concern to others, but *equal* concern. Thus: 'The responsibilities a true [as opposed to a bare] community deploys are special and individualised and display a pervasive mutual concern that fits a plausible conception of equal concern.'[26] Now a community that adopts 'law as integrity' – a community whose legal rights and duties must all conform to one 'scheme of justice' or one 'set of principles' – gives rise, says Dworkin, to a form of law which satisfies the requirements of true associative obligations. He says:

> The model of principle makes the responsibilities of citizenship special ... It commands that nobody be left out, that we are all in politics together for better or worse, that no one may be sacrificed, like wounded left in the battlefield, to the crusade for justice overall. The concern it expresses is not shallow, like the crocodile concern of the rulebook model, but genuine and pervasive ... Everyone's political acts express on every occasion ... a deep and constant commitment commanding sacrifice, not just by losers but also by the powerful who would gain by the kind of logrolling and checkerboard solutions integrity forbids. Its rationale tends toward equality ... its command ... assumes that each person is as worthy as any other, that each must be treated with equal concern according to some coherent conception of what that means.[27]

Amen! This litany, this well-nigh emotional outpouring, is, as it stands, completely mysterious. Not one word is said about how all these wonderful virtues are achieved by integrity. Still, we can somehow divine where all these virtues might come from (though the link with integrity remains as incomprehensible as ever): these virtues might be brought about by prohibiting our laws from manifesting moral 'double standards'; from the idea that the law must judge everybody according to the same moral principles – which is, of course, the problem that Dworkin sees all along in checkerboard statutes (which he describes as employing one moral principle for one group and another for another group). But, once more, Dworkin mistakes one phenomenon for another: he seems to believe that the prohibition on double standards and the requirements of integrity amount to one and the same thing. This is one more formulation of the presumed – and unjustified – identity we examined before between the arbitrariness of checkerboard statutes and the arbitrariness of employing different 'schemes of justice'; and like its predecessor, this identity is at best in need of serious argumentation, and at worst a simple mistake.

Avoiding double standards, as far as that expression pertains to an unreasonable moral position, requires that the same set of moral principles be applied to those *similarly situated* – but not that it be applied to all groups, whoever they are, for whatever purpose, and all over the place (which is what integrity appears to demand). If I claim that drug dealers should get stiff jail sentences but that my son, caught selling drugs, should not, I employ a double

---

26 Dworkin, 1986, p 201.
27 Dworkin, 1986, p 213.

standard: my son and other drug dealers are similarly situated and they therefore deserve similar treatment according to the same moral standard. But I do not employ a double standard – at least not in a sense that is readily recognised as morally unacceptable – if I believe that drug dealers should get stiff jail sentences because I employ some strict utilitarian calculation, and I also claim that the government may not prohibit the use of condoms because I think this would be a violation of some human rights theory – *even if the two theories point to different resolutions to these and other questions and appear to be irreconcilable*. The idea that it is morally unacceptable to employ, for different moral questions, different and potentially conflicting moral theories, is just bizarre. Of course, Dworkin is free to claim that to do so constitutes an injury to equality and equal concern; but he must tell us why this is so. Employing different and possibly irreconcilable sets of moral principles on different occasions is something people do all the time, and do not consider to be 'wrong'. So the prohibition on the employment of moral double standards in the law – and all the wonderful consequences deriving from it – seems to have little to do with Dworkin's idea of integrity. Once separated from the false support of our checkerboard instincts, integrity appears to possess no desirable attributes of its own.

So what is integrity anyway?

Integrity, says Dworkin, demands that our laws 'speak with one voice' – that is, that they all conform to one 'set of principles' or one 'scheme of justice'. But what does it mean to employ one 'scheme of justice' or one 'set of principles'? As we saw, one formulation Dworkin gives is simply this: a 'scheme of justice' manifests a certain fixed ranking of moral principles. So long as this particular ranking is preserved, we are dealing with one and the same 'moral scheme'.[28] But Dworkin also claims that the prohibition of abortion conforms to the same 'scheme of justice' as allowing abortion for women impregnated by rape. This appears quite counter-intuitive, for these two legal rules (the one prohibiting abortion and the other excepting rape-caused pregnancies) seem to represent reverse rankings of moral principles – one rule prioritising the preservation of life over women's autonomy, the other prioritising autonomy over the preservation of life.[29] Of course, Dworkin can hardly characterise such a legal

---

28 See Dworkin, 1986, p 184; p 436 (fn 7).

29 The difference between pregnancies caused by rape and other pregnancies involves the degree to which the pregnant woman is responsible for her pregnancy, and, conceivably, the degree to which the baby is unwanted. These factors – which may justify allowing abortion in non-rape-caused pregnancies just as well – simply reach greater prominence in the case of rapes. There does not seem to be a *further* or different principle that explains why rape-caused pregnancies are to be exempted while all other pregnancies are not: it is simply a matter of reaching a point where the tables turn – where the priorities among the principles of preservation of life and autonomy are flipped because the disadvantages of being deprived of autonomy reach intolerable levels. In any case it does not appear that a person adopting this moral position would feel in the least obliged (assuming he is [cont]

scheme as a violation of integrity: it seems to represent a perfectly acceptable moral and legal position. But the idea that such a legal scheme can be said to conform to one 'scheme of justice' does not make it easy to understand what Dworkin means by that term.

The difficulty does not end here, even if we grant that the rape-pregnancy exception and the prohibition of abortion somehow *do* conform to one and the same 'scheme of justice' or 'ranked set of principles'. For integrity would now demand that this ranking be maintained throughout the law. If a legal scheme manifests a certain ranking of two principles, then integrity is preserved only so long as these two principles receive the same ranking in other legal schemes: presumably, integrity would be violated if a subsequent legal scheme manifests exclusive preference for one of those principles and utter neglect of the other. (Put differently, the claim insists that the same moral reasons must be equally respected in all our laws.) But understood literally this way, integrity is certainly absent from our law: laws habitually present ranking among principles which other laws flout altogether (or, put differently again, it is habitually the case that some laws respect moral reasons which other laws do not). Indeed, why shouldn't they? The income tax scheme represents a ranking of the two principles that a man has a right to the fruits of his labour, and that people with many fruits ought to share them with the have-nots. But competition law dispenses with the second principle altogether: immensely profitable supermarket mega-chains are permitted to open shop next to poor grocers and swiftly drive them to destitution (though both our moral principles are certainly relevant to this legal scheme).[30] This, of course, is an absurd example: Dworkin could not have meant that integrity is violated here. But the example is brought as a caution against too facile a reading of Dworkin's claims. We cannot content ourselves with slogans: any legal scheme can be said to conform to a number of moral principles, and the claim that all schemes must manifest the same ranking of principles would be downright wrong if we were not to give it a less literal formulation. We must endow the requirement of an 'equal ranking of principles throughout' with a more substantive understanding; but what could such an understanding be?

---

29 [cont] not teaching moral philosophy) to come up with such a further moral principle explaining this presumed flipping of priorities – nothing above the simple claim that, in rape-caused pregnancies, prohibiting abortion becomes too injurious both for the potential mother and for the potential newborn.

30 This complaint is equally applicable to moral *theories* – a utilitarian and a right-based theory, for example – for these, too, are moral reasons or principles only brought to an organising level of greater abstraction. Consider the law allowing the state to forcibly draft people at a time of war and ship them to the front. This law conforms to the utilitarian principle that the welfare of the many justifies the sacrifice of the welfare of the few. Yet other legal schemes – like the one guaranteeing the freedom of expression for some highly offensive speech – conform to principles setting a limit to the demands a community can make on its individuals in the name of overall utility. Does Dworkin mean to say that the coexistence of these two laws spells a violation of integrity? That these theories must be respected *in the same way* throughout the law? If he does, then integrity surely does not fit the legal materials; if he doesn't, we need a different explanation of what that requirement means.

Dworkin's examples of integrity in action are of surprisingly little help here – for, as it comes out, they pay no attention to integrity. For instance, Dworkin says that failing to recognise the principle of a right for compensation for emotional injury would be a mistake because 'No one who believed that people never have rights to compensation for emotional injury could have reached the results of those past decisions cited in McLoughlin that allowed compensation'.[31] This principle – like all others Dworkin cites – is not even checked for agreement with the principles to which other laws conform; it is recognised as a valid legal principle simply because it accords with the precedents most on point. This good-old-fashioned legal analysis says nothing at all about any set of principles respected throughout the law. But while the precedents most on point may be very clear on the issue of emotional damages, it is surely possible that their underlying principle does not belong to the set of principles to which all other laws conform.

The closest that Dworkin's examples ever get to concerning themselves with the law as a whole is by inquiring into the principles underlying similar doctrines of tort law when no decisive answer is found in the cases most on point. But this may mean very little to the value of integrity: legal interpreters may examine solutions to similar problems (they often do) without bothering at all with whether solutions to *other* problems also conform to an identical 'scheme of justice'. The entire point of integrity is that only *certain* moral principles are legally relevant – the moral principles which *are equally respected throughout the law*.[32] Surely the fact that a certain moral principle underlies the most relevant precedent does not mean it is respected throughout the law. And if the only way flesh and blood judges can operate consists in employing the moral principles of the most relevant cases (without inquiring into the law as a whole) – well, so much the worse for integrity! For judges, it seems, may faithfully operate in accordance with this methodology while violating integrity in each and every one of their cases: that methodology does not and cannot show the slightest concern with integrity. On the complaint that judges, being human, simply cannot construct a set of principles respected throughout the law – as Dworkin's mythical judge Hercules does – Dworkin says that it 'misunderstands the exercise': 'Hercules does what they would do if they had a career to devote to a single decision; they need, not a different conception of law from his, but skills of craft husbandry and efficiency he has never had to cultivate.'[33] This response is highly unsatisfactory. What it means is that judges must attribute legal validity to moral principles which may or may not be respected throughout the law. In what way, then, does Hercules – who

---

31 Dworkin, 1986, p 242.

32 In fact this requirement, which obviously lies at the very heart of integrity's demands, is at times explicitly played down by Dworkin himself: 'Integrity requires [Hercules] to construct, for each statute he is asked to enforce, some justification that fits and flows through that statute and is, *if possible*, consistent with other legislation in force.' Dworkin, 1986, p 338 (emphasis added). What if it is not? What does integrity require then?

33 Dworkin, 1986, p 265.

attributes legal validity only to the former principles – 'show us the hidden structure of their judgments and so lays these open to study and criticism'?[34] The judges in Dworkin's examples do not even try to do what Hercules does: their guiding conception is different altogether.

Nor can we advance our understanding of integrity's requirements by reflecting on Dworkin's repetitive assertions that a 'set of principles' must maintain the moral coherency of *an individual*. This insistence appears, among many other places, in Dworkin's discussion of integrity's affinity with the ideal of self-legislation. Integrity, says Dworkin, allows citizens to see themselves as the hypothetical authors of the law; the ideal of self-legislation 'needs integrity … for a citizen cannot treat himself as the author of a collection of laws that are inconsistent in principle'.[35] What integrity demands is that our laws be justified according to a single 'set of principles' such as one individual can hold: 'The adjudicative principle of integrity instructs judges to identify legal rights and duties, so far as possible, on the assumption that they were all created by a single person – the community personified …'[36] In short, when we examine whether any two laws conform to the same 'set of principles' we must ask ourselves whether the moral principles informing these laws can coexist in one individual. But this is entirely unhelpful, if only because individuals can and do hold any conceivable set of moral principles.[37] I may think it contradictory to believe in the right to commit suicide while denying the right for assisted suicide, but some people believe just that: I personally met one recently. The quality shared by all and only sets of principles that one individual can hold remains totally incomprehensible.

To make a long story short, as hard as one tries one cannot grasp integrity's requirement: one knows integrity requires that all our laws conform to one 'set of principles' or one 'scheme of justice'; but one gets nowhere in trying to understand in what sense this is a limiting condition, for it seems that any combination of moral principles would do. Nor can one understand the idea of a consistent application of a set of principles *throughout*: read literally this requirement is absurd, but how else should one read it?[38] This point lies at the

---

34 Dworkin, 1986, p 265.
35 Dworkin, 1986, p 189. This, by the way, is supposedly another desirable attribute of integrity (though it is hard to see in what sense a person can see himself as the author of a collection of laws which conform to moral principles with which he may vehemently disagree).
36 Dworkin, 1986, p 225. See also Dworkin, 1986, p 229, where Dworkin analogises the requirements of integrity to the writing of a chain novel, saying of the authors in the chain that they 'must try to make this the best novel it can be construed as the work of a single author rather than, as is the fact, the product of many different hands'.
37 Sigmund Freud believed that individuals often hold sets of beliefs that they *themselves* recognise as incoherent: see Freud, 1966, p 94. See also Benjamin, 1990, pp 20–22.
38 The whole point can be put another way: integrity requires principled legal solutions, which Dworkin contrasts with internally compromised ones. Principled solutions supposedly offer an external, rather than an internal, compromise. The claim I am making is that this latter distinction is vacuous.

heart of much of the criticism levelled against Dworkin over the years.[39] Take, for example, the simple complaint, found in an article by John Mackie, that Dworkin's interpretive theory 'is a plea for a more speculative and enterprising handling by judges of their traditional materials and data'.[40] In answering the charge Dworkin replies that Mackie's is 'a political objection': Mackie thinks, says Dworkin 'that my theory will increase deception [when compared to positivistic theories, Mackie's preferred alternatives], because judges will pretend that they are finding determinate solutions to legal issues when they are really legislating their personal convictions'.[41] The objection is presumably political because it alleges that the judicial branch will exercise illegitimate power through deception when sanctioned to employ controversial criteria (which 'law as integrity' indeed necessitates): the necessary controversiality of the decision-making process will make deception more common by making it more difficult to detect. Dworkin then rejects the charge by claiming that deception is as much a possibility – if not more so – under a positivistic conception of law.

But I do not think that Mackie is concerned with deception. Mackie's complaint is not that judges will find it easier to deceive (though this does appear to be true);[42] the concern I believe Mackie is expressing is that judges may do their very honest and intellectual best to arrive at legal solutions according to 'law as integrity' and still legislate their personal convictions for lack of anything else. Since the sense with which integrity is supposed to guide legal determinations is a mystery (hence the inexorably 'speculative' nature of the judges' efforts), the problem is not that judges (willingly or not) may go wrong, but that there is no sense in which they can go right. 'Integrity' is a theoretical notion meaning to offer a sense of some desirable overall coherence among legal rights and duties; but it fails to fulfil this promise: that overall coherence is a chimera – a theoretical requirement which, once examined closely, dissolves before our eyes.

The real mystery

But then we are faced with a second and perhaps larger mystery: why would Dworkin – or anybody else for that matter – hypothesise a political and moral value whose theoretical requirements are incomprehensible, and whose moral and political merit is utterly unclear? Why on earth would anybody claim that legal interpretation aspires, and should aspire, to a characteristic whose

---

39 See, eg, Raz, 1992, pp 317–21 (where Raz details the different senses of 'coherence' that Dworkin associates with the notion of integrity).

40 Mackie, 1984, p 169. Mackie criticises Dworkin's ideas as they are expressed in Dworkin's *Taking Rights Seriously* – not in *Law's Empire*, the book upon which I concentrate. But his point is equally applicable to the theory laid down in this latter book.

41 Dworkin, 1984, pp 272–74.

42 Where a judge must follow conventional linguistic rules rather than follow controversial moral judgments, deception becomes 'harder' in the sense that it is more easily detected.

requirements are an enigma, whose desirability is unexplainable, and whose pursuit is in any case beyond the methodological reaches of flesh and blood judges? The answer lies with a virtue Dworkin believes integrity possesses which is, strictly speaking, neither moral nor political: it is the virtue of making possible *one* correct legal answer. In integrity Dworkin is hypothesising a constraint which is supposed to narrow the various possibilities of legal interpretation effectively to one: integrity is the structural requirement which generates one correct legal result.

Judges, says Dworkin, must look upon themselves as writers in a chain novel, writing a chapter in a book whose previous chapters were written by others. As the book progresses – as it becomes richer in detail – the possibilities of correct progression become more and more limited: 'If you have been given almost all of *A Christmas Carol* with only the very end to be written – Scrooge has already had his dreams, repented, and sent his turkey – it is too late for you to make him irredeemably wicked, assuming you think, as most interpreters would, that the text will not bear that interpretation without too much strain ...'[43] The same goes for legal interpretation when guided by the ideal of integrity: interpretations are more and more constrained the more data they have, when they are guided by a principle demanding some coherent integration of all the legal materials.[44] When the wealth of the legal materials reaches a certain level, many answers to legal questions are bad, some are tolerable, and one is 'correct': this is the right legal answer. Indeed integrity has a long history in Dworkin's writing, and its articulation in *Law's Empire* is an attempt to give some more theoretical grounding to the famous 'right answer' thesis. The attempt, as we saw, fails: what integrity is, and how it constrains legal interpretation, is a Chinese puzzle. Still, the idea that the law is the set of propositions conforming to the moral scheme that best fits our institutional legal materials and puts them in their best light desperately needs integrity – with its promise of one correct legal answer – in order to offer a palatable conception of law.

II Integrity and impartiality

Dworkin's response

The thing that makes law with one correct legal answer so palatable is the possibility of impartial legal interpretation: so long as the law uniquely determines the resolution of a case, and the practitioner follows the law, there

---

43 Dworkin, 1986, p 232.

44 For a rejection of this claim as it appears in Dworkin's earlier writings, see Fish, 1982, p 554. ('It is of course tempting to think that the more information one has (the more history) the more directed will be one's interpretation; but information only comes in an interpreted form (it does not announce itself). No matter how much or how little you have, it cannot be a check against interpretation because even when you first "see" it, interpretation has already done its work.') See also Fish, 1983.

is no danger of partiality as far as legal interpretation is concerned. According to Dworkin, the law is the set of propositions conforming to the moral scheme that best fits the legal materials and puts them in their best light; and it follows, presumably, that there is one right answer for most legal questions. There is no guarantee, of course, that any legal interpreter would reach that answer; but such are the limitations of mortals: they struggle, within their earthly confines, to perform as best as they can. The methodology required by 'law as integrity' (as Dworkin readily acknowledges) requires the judge to consult her personal opinions over moral matters; this is a necessary part of the effort to arrive at the correct legal answer. However, if the judge is right then these opinions are not 'personal' after all but are valid for all, for there is a correct set of moral principles that best fits the legal materials and puts them in their best light. Since the law is in principle fully determinate, partiality in legal application can only be the result of the legal interpreter's failure to hit upon the correct legal answer – that is to say, the result of bad faith or error. But there is nothing we can do to eliminate these two as possibilities: whatever theory of law we may come up with, bad faith and error will always pose a threat to impartiality.

The problem of impartiality in legal interpretation often appears as the problem of the objectivity or the subjectivity of that process (subjective legal interpretation being decision-making with no universal validity), the danger being legal interpretation that to one extent or another is indelibly subjective. Dworkin seeks to shift the entire terms of this debate: all legal questions have one correct answer measured against universally valid criteria (these criteria being the coherency required by integrity); the only real problem is getting to that answer. Judges must employ some controversial 'personal' opinions in ascertaining legal rights and duties; but these opinions do not *decide* what these legal rights and duties really are: the correct legal rights and duties exist, so to speak, independently of these opinions. There is no problem of indelible subjectivity with legal interpretation, only a problem with getting things right; and this is a problem from which no human inquiry is free, and certainly not a concern that is unique to the law.

This supposedly shifts the focus of our concern: we no longer need to worry about the indeterminacy of legal interpretation; we only need to worry about how to get these interpretations right, and who is most likely to do this. So when Mackie claims that the problem with Dworkin's theory is that it 'is a plea for a more speculative and enterprising handling by judges of their traditional materials and data', Dworkin claims that Mackie's objection is based on an open political question – viz, whether judges will deceive more if they can employ controversial considerations.[45] It is *not* an open political question, of course, whether it should be judges or other officials who select controversial legal requirements from among the available legislative alternatives: such determinations, everyone agrees, are the business of elected representatives.

---

45 Mackie, 1984, p 169.

What *is* an open political question, presumably, is whether once such choices are made, judges ought to be able to employ 'more speculative and enterprising' considerations in ascertaining their proper legal consequences. Mackie was making his objection believing that a 'more speculative and enterprising' legal interpretation is clearly something to be avoided; but this is precisely what Dworkin denies: a 'more speculative and enterprising' legal interpretation is to be avoided only if we think that it will lead to more deception on the part of judges. Perhaps the best way to operate our legal system is to let judges be more speculative and enterprising because this is the best way to get them to the correct answers. This change of focus is based on the claim that there is one correct answer to any legal question.

A good response?

One edifying way in which to evaluate the significance of Dworkin's presumed solution to the partiality problem is to compare it to another solution that is generally discredited today – the solution offered by the theory of natural law. According to natural law theory, legal interpretation is guided by certain universal moral truths which are accessible to man. So at least as far as moral preferences are used in the process, natural law theory maintains – as does 'law as integrity' – that partial legal interpretation can only be the result of a failure – either innocent or deliberate – to practise legal interpretation correctly. Why does natural law theory seem to fail? Why is it such an unpalatable theory for most people today? There are two possible answers to this question. The first answer is philosophical (or metaphysical): there may be no universal moral truths. If things are so then the solution offered obviously collapses. The analogy to 'law as integrity' would be the failure of integrity to produce one correct legal solution. If integrity cannot do that job – and from what we have seen there is no reason to think that it can – then Dworkin's theory does nothing to alleviate our concern.

But natural law theory – and 'law as integrity' – may also suffer from an incurable practical (or epistemological) difficulty: whether there are or aren't any universal moral truths, the mere fact that reasonable people disagree about these truths is enough to make natural law's response to the impartiality problem unworkable. Most people who find natural law theory unsatisfactory never concern themselves with such high-flown philosophical questions as the existence of universally valid moral truths; they find it sufficient that reasonable people habitually and pervasively disagree about certain moral propositions, and that no consensus has ever developed around many central moral disputes. These people see the problem of impartiality in the law as practical through and through: the question of 'correct' answers is meaningful for the impartiality problem only to the extent it concerns what we agree is correct – not what is correct independently of our disagreements. If a consideration that decides a case is controversial such that reasonable and well informed people are bound to disagree about its veracity, then that consideration implicates the problem of partiality whether it is or is not true.

It is easy to see why things are so: as we saw, considerations of preference are controversial, and they also tend to reflect the self-interest of the people, or groups of people, who hold them.[46] These two conditions remain whether those considerations of preference do or do not have truth-values. (Put differently, we are still left with the following problem: people's preferences are often false; and their falseness may accumulate in a rather peculiar way, that is, on the side of the decision-maker's interests.) So even if we assume that Dworkin is right in his claim that integrity secures one correct answer to any legal question (and we have seen no good reason to do that), this success is entirely hollow: if judges must use controversial personal preferences in seeking to arrive at a legal solution – as Dworkin readily acknowledges they must – then the problem of impartiality remains unsolved. Who cares that these personal opinions may be somehow 'correct' if we all hold contradictory views of which ones are? It is enough that judges use these controversial preferences to decide cases, whether these – from some Herculean point of view – are 'correct' or not. It is for this reason that Hart's theory, if it were correct, would have alleviated our concern over impartiality – whereas Dworkin's solution, even were it correct, would not. Determinate law solves the partiality problem only to the extent to which it excludes considerations of preference – whether these are defined as beliefs lacking a truth-value or as highly and chronically controversial. If our legal interpretation sanctions the habitual use of such considerations, then its determinacy is a thesis whose interest is limited to academic metaphysicians and their opponents: impartiality needs to be publicly seen, not philosophically pledged. Dworkin may believe he is making an important point when he argues that legal solutions have one correct legal answer. This is a significant assertion as far as controversies between legal theorists go. But it is an assertion with few practical implications for the question of impartiality, or for all those issues (judicial discretion, for instance, or the problem of moral evaluation in legal application) which derive their significance from it.

---

46 See Chapter 1.

Chapter 6
Law and reason: beyond impartiality

1 Legislation

I have tried to demonstrate that both Dworkin and Hart were devising theories of law seeking to portray proper legal interpretation as necessarily impartial. The following conception of law has no such ambition; in fact, it presents a picture of legal interpretation where some legal questions *must* be answered by the use of preferences. Partiality, according to this understanding, is sometimes *unavoidable* in perfectly valid legal determinations. But the thrust of this conception is not critical: it is an exploration of the constraints which guide and constrict legal interpretation – even though these constraints do not eliminate partiality. Nevertheless, the concern over partiality remains, of course, looming above: to speak of the constraints of legal interpretation is to speak of the curbing of discretion and its potential for partiality; and the degree to which these constraints preclude or permit partial decision-making remains an important measure in evaluating their significance.

The principle of public reason

I would like to go back to Dworkin's puzzling question regarding checkerboard statutes:

> Do the people of North Dakota disagree whether justice requires compensation for product defects that manufacturers could not reasonably have prevented? Then why should their legislature not impose this 'strict' liability on manufacturers of automobiles but not on manufacturers of washing machines? Do the people of Alabama disagree about the morality of racial discrimination? Why should their legislature not forbid racial discrimination on buses but permit it in restaurants? Do the British divide on the morality of abortions? Why should Parliament not make abortions criminal for pregnant women who were born on even years but not for those born in odd ones?[1]

We all feel, of course, that these suggestions are unacceptable; the question is why, and whether this has any significance to legal practice. As we saw, Dworkin believes the explanation lies in our demand that all legal requirements derive from one 'scheme of justice' or one 'set of moral principles'.[2] Having seen that this proposal gets nowhere, we should reopen

---

1 Dworkin, 1986, p 178.

2 'The most natural explanation of why we oppose checkerboard statutes appeals to [integrity]: we say that a state that adopts these internal compromises is acting in an unprincipled way ... [I]t must endorse principles to justify part of what it has done that it must reject to justify the rest.' Dworkin, 1986, pp 183–84.

the question of what distinguishes checkerboard statutes (for example, a statute allowing abortions to women born in odd but not even years) from *non*-checkerboard statutes (for example, a statute making abortions criminal for pregnant women but not for women impregnated by rape); for with his checkerboard statutes Dworkin has touched on a point that is crucial for the understanding of modern law.

Now as we saw above, it seems that the essential difference between the two statutes lies in the fact that in the checkerboard statute (the one permitting abortions to women born in odd years but not to women born in even ones) we do not see any reason for treating these two classes differently, while in the case of the regulation prohibiting abortions to all women but those impregnated by rape we *do* recognise reasons as to why these two classes may be treated differently (the total lack of responsibility for the pregnancy, the degree to which the newborn is unwanted, and so on). We do not have to *endorse* this reason in order to distinguish this statute from the checkerboard statute: we may think, for instance, that rape does *not* justify an abortion. Still, we see that this statute has some reason for the distinction it makes. (I shall return to this important point below.) Thus it appears that we expect to identify a reason as to why a statute treats two seemingly similar categories differently, and with checkerboard statutes there seems to be no such reason (no reason as to why to treat differently women born in odd years and women born in even years in regulating abortions, no reason for treating manufacturers of washing machines differently from car manufacturers in product liability regulation, no reason for treating discrimination on buses differently from discrimination in restaurants). Checkerboard statutes prescribe one legal requirement to one class and a second legal requirement to another while the difference between the two classes does not explain that difference in treatment. This expectation is commonly expressed in the idea of 'equality before the law': the similarly situated are to be treated similarly. This is not merely a *formal* adjudicative principle (where some positive law *defines* the similarly situated); it is a substantive legislative principle as well. A criminal statute which applies to those whose last names begin with the letters A to N but not to those whose last names begin with O to Z would violate our idea of equality before the law; for we can see no reason as to why an act is criminal if committed by those whose names begin with the first letters of the alphabet, but legal if committed by those whose names begin with the last. We expect statutes to have a publicly recognisable reason for the distinctions that they make.[3]

---

3 Note that the reasons that we expect statutes to have need not be easy to detect: it may take some work to unearth them. The rules governing secured transactions, for example, form a complex and interrelated system of regulations; and it may take some effort to figure out why a statute distinguishes between leases with, and leases without, an unlimited option to terminate. A similar effort must go into detecting the public justification of a statute like the US Commodity Futures Modernization Act of 2000, which exempts trading in energy from the regulatory scrutiny applied to brokers of money, securities, and commodities. (Pub L No 106-554, 114 Stat 2763 (2000), [cont]

The relation between the category and the treatment

In raising the question of checkerboard statutes Dworkin in fact hypothesises a reason for the distinctions these statutes make: these distinctions are the result of legislative compromises – of the wish to accommodate seemingly valid but conflicting opinions (for instance, one opinion calling for the freedom to abort and another calling for its prohibition). Now why can't this explanation furnish the required reason for the different treatments accorded by these statutes? It cannot because the different treatments it is supposed to explain *have nothing to do with the features of the distinguished categories*: we expect that any difference in treatment be *a function of* the dissimilarity between the differently treated classes (or 'have something to do with' the dissimilarity, or 'be related to' it, or 'be connected with' it, or any such number of formulations). When a statute forbids abortion to all women but those impregnated by rape, the prescribed difference in treatment has something to do with the distinction between being impregnated so to speak 'normally' and being impregnated by rape. Similarly, when the prohibition of abortion is held applicable to women born in odd but not in even years, the prescribed difference in treatment must have something to do with the difference between being born in an odd year and being born in an even one. We expect to discern a justification as to what made the legislature draw the *specific* distinctions it did. Dworkin's hypothesised reason does not explain why *these specific* categories (women born in even years and women born in odd years) are treated the way that they are; in fact, under Dworkin's hypothesis there is no such reason – the two categories are, presumably, arbitrarily chosen. If you ask me to explain why I treat white chickens more kindly then brown chickens and I respond 'because I have mixed feelings about chickens' I haven't explained the very distinction I make between chickens that are white and chickens that

---

3   [cont] codified in scattered parts of the United States Code.) The distinction between energy commodities and other commodities – like the difference between leases with or without unlimited options to terminate – is, presumably, what lies beneath this difference in treatment; but that distinction is not immediately apparent, and its articulation may require some work. Another example is a statute which prohibits under-surface digging in a certain specified area. The public reason underlying this statute is not immediately apparent; yet this statute doesn't appear to us as a checkerboard statute. These three examples have what may be called a 'colourable' claim for a public justification: they do not appear to us as checkerboard statutes because, looking at the distinctions they draw, we presume that the required justification *does exist*.

But this need not mean that they are not *in fact* checkerboard statutes: Dworkin's examples present us with categories where the possibility of a justification is basically nil (distinguishing between those born in even and those born in odd years for purposes of the regulation of abortion does not have even a remotely colourable claim for a justification); but what Dworkin's examples teach us also extends to statutes with *colourable* claims: ie, that if these colourable claims turn out to be empty promises, then we would reject these statutes as well – and for the very same reasons we reject Dworkin's checkerboard statutes. (Indeed, this seemed to be the exact problem with the US Commodity Futures Modernization Act.) *And* the question whether they are or are not empty promises must be answerable, in principle, by anybody wishing to ascertain it: that answer must be publicly available.

are brown. The situation here is similar: what *we* seek a reason for is why the statute calls for a treatment of this *particular* category that is different from the treatment of that *particular* one. The response that 'this is a compromise between pro- and anti-abortion legislators' supplies no such reason.

Why do we demand that the reason for a statutory distinction be derived from the characteristics of the distinguished classes? This is a fundamental limitation on power that is imposed by the form of a legal order; and it is aimed both at guaranteeing the rationality of legal regulations and at making the reasons for legal regulations publicly available: a legal system is essentially a system of regulation grounded in publicly recognised reasons.

Arbitrary distinctions?

Now these claims could be proved wrong if there were perfectly acceptable laws having arbitrary distinctions. Dworkin, whose understanding of checkerboard statutes is different from the one proposed here (but for whom arbitrary distinctions would have also proved a problem), concedes that some laws *do* draw arbitrary distinctions – 'we do accept arbitrary distinctions about some matters: zoning, for example' – but he adds that arbitrary distinctions are *not* acceptable where issues of justice are concerned.[4] But I think there is little reason for this concession: allowing that many laws exhibit some inevitable measure of arbitrariness because of their *line-drawing* (for example, when the driving age is set at 17 rather than at 17 and one month), zoning ordinances exhibit just such arbitrariness and not more: given the need to draw *some line* between one geographic area and another, the arbitrariness inherent in zoning schemes is no greater than the one in a law setting a minimum age for driving. To put things in the terms I employed above, the different treatment accorded to different zones is not unrelated to the dissimilarities between these zones. Zoning is a well planned activity taking into account the various differences between different geographical areas (the number of residents, original character of the zone, its centrality, and so on), and it is simply wrong to think that no justification, having to do with the difference between the zones, can explain the different treatments accorded to them. We would certainly consider unacceptable any zoning scheme that delineated its sectors arbitrarily – one dividing urban space by drawing random geometrical patterns, for example.

Take another statute drawing a seemingly arbitrary distinction: a law aimed at reducing pollution and traffic by allowing vehicles with *odd* registration numbers to be operated only Sunday through Wednesday, and those with *even* numbers to operate Wednesday through Saturday. Isn't *this* an arbitrary (though perfectly sensible) statutory line-drawing? The answer, once again, is that it is not: an arbitrary distinction carves up two categories whose difference

---

4   Dworkin denies that such arbitrary distinctions contradict his claim (that we expect all our laws to derive from one scheme of justice) by denying that these statutes raise any question of principle – that is, they do not involve questions of justice: '... But we reject a division between parties of opinion when matters of principle are at stake.' Dworkin, 1986, p 179.

cannot account for the different treatments they receive; but the distinction between odd and even registration numbers *does* account for the difference in treatment. The distinction between cars with odd and even registration numbers is a distinction between two groups having the same number of cars, having a roughly similar geographic distribution, where the ratio of family cars or trucks is roughly the same, and so on. This distinction is a proxy for two well defined (and presumably similar) categories; and the treatment prescribed for these two essentially similar pools is also essentially similar (the difference merely being the days of the week in which they may operate). The distinction between even and odd registration numbers is, in this respect, not an arbitrary distinction: it is a distinction which captures two well defined categories of vehicles. If it turned out that it did not – for example, if it emerged that all family cars have odd registration numbers, or that all trucks have even ones – then that statute would be as objectionable as any other checkerboard statute. There is no good reason to concede that the law draws arbitrary distinctions: it does not.[5]

Recharacterising the problem with checkerboard statutes

Now the problem with checkerboard statutes can be better perceived if we stop talking about 'equal treatment' and start talking about the statutory requirement itself. Here is what I mean: the problem with Dworkin's checkerboard abortion statute is not merely the lack of a reason for treating women born in even and those born in odd years unequally; it is the lack of a reason for prohibiting abortions *to the category of women born in even years*. We seek a reason, related to the features of the category singled out by the statute, as to why that category is treated as the statute demands.[6] We may have a reason as to why to prohibit abortion to *all women*; but we have no reason as to why to prohibit it to women *born in even years*: we seek a reason as to why the specifically defined operative category is treated the way that it is. The fact

---

5   There are rare cases where we actively seek a measure of *randomness* (and where the preference for the random therefore supplies some of the required justification for the distinction made by a statute). Statutes regulating jury selection are such an example: they devise a random mechanism for the choice of juries, and, within well defined limits, the more random the process, the better. But these are, once more, well defined limits indeed: laws may aim at randomness, but never at arbitrariness. A jury selection statute – like the licence plate statute we just examined – applies to categories with certain sought-after features having to do with its prescribed treatment (for example, a representative distribution of racial or economic status).

6   For the purposes of this discussion there can be no significant distinction between a general rule and an exception. The general rule merely constitutes the background conditions against which the exception defines the legal requirement. Thus, the exception for rape-caused pregnancies may be equally described not as an exception but as the granting of a legal privilege to abort. The requirement of rationality would remain the same: there must be a relation between the features defining our operative category and the legal requirement (or, in this context, the legal privilege) mandated by the law. What is being signalled by an exception is the idea that the operative category is explained both with, *but also without*, the excluded class.

that there may be a reason for mandating that all stores be closed on Sundays does not mean that there is a reason for mandating that all shoe stores be closed. If our operative category is 'males 18–21 years of age with a physical disability' then the reason we seek is not only as to why treat males the way the statute requires, nor only why treat males '18–21 years of age' that way; we also want a reason for specifying the physical disability.[7]

In short, one need not look upon the problem of checkerboard statutes as the lack of *equal treatment* for two similarly situated groups: we are offended by checkerboard statutes because we identify no recognisable reason, having to do with the features of these statutes' operative category (women born in even years, manufacturers of washing machines, and so on), as to why the state treats that category the way the statute demands. The problem is one of explanation – not, strictly speaking, of equality.[8]

Unreasonable reasons

Now what counts as a proper explanation – that is to say, as a 'recognisable reason'? As I noted above, and as Dworkin also recognises, we need not *endorse* a reason in order that it satisfy our demand: we may recognise a reason as sufficient even if we do not accept it as a good one. (Dworkin says that a law prohibiting abortions which exempts pregnancies caused by rape would not be regarded as a checkerboard statute even by those who think that rape does not justify an abortion.[9]) The perspective from which one judges whether a statute is or is not supported by a public reason is not restricted to one's own understanding, but encompasses opinions that may very well contradict one's own.[10] This perspective, however, has its obvious limits: if we are looking for

---

7   There need not be only *one* reason accounting for the different features of our operative category: we may have distinct reasons for different features. This is the case in the statute prohibiting abortions to 'all women not impregnated by rape': the reason for prohibiting abortions to women (having to do with the protection of human life) is independent of the reason for prohibiting abortions only to those not impregnated by rape (having to do with the circumstances of a forced impregnation outweighing our initial concern). So the reason need not be one, but all the defining features of the operative category must be accounted for.

8   In any case, if there must be a reason, having to do with the distinction between two seemingly similar categories, as to why one category receives one treatment and a second category another, there must also be a reason as to why the operative category receives the treatment that it does. It is only in light of this *latter* reason that the reason justifying the different treatments can exist.

9   See Dworkin, 1986, p 183.

10   Note that the public reasons we expect our laws to possess may derive from any corner of human understanding: scientific knowledge, economic theories, sociological studies, political and moral opinions, even religious beliefs. (In contrast, Dworkin sees in checkerboard statutes only *moral* arbitrariness.) The reason for the exception allowing abortions for women impregnated by rape is an example of a morally informed explanation. A law requiring people to be dressed modestly when entering public shrines derives its reason from religious understanding. The essential point about those reasons is that they exist, so to speak, independently of the law.

reasons, then particularly *bad* reasons (or *'unreasonable* reasons', if I may use this awkward but adequate expression) cannot do.[11] We recognise some opinions incompatible with our own as valid opinions (saying to ourselves: 'well, this is certainly not *my* opinion on the matter, but I can accept it as a legitimate one'); but there are opinions which simply do not appear to us valid.

For example, many people think that there is a relation between the position of the planets at the time of one's birth and one's psychological makeup. This opinion may be popular, but it clashes with some pretty solid ideas many of us have, and a statute based upon it will strike many of us as lacking a reasonable explanation (imagine a statute granting certain employment preferences for those born between 11 March and 13 May). A statute confining Jews or Blacks to certain geographical areas similarly lacks a reasonable explanation for its treatment of its operative category – although some nasty characters are sure to recognise one. Such opinions are thought to conflict with some of our more solid moral beliefs, and they can no longer be accepted as 'reasons'. Thus, what at one point may have appeared a perfectly acceptable statute would have been transformed, by changes in moral attitudes, into a checkerboard statute – an offence to our legal sensibilities and our understanding of what can and what cannot constitute a law. In short, we see some positions as too unmistakably false, or as conflicting with ideas we think too well defended, and we will not accept these as sufficient explanations.

Now whether an opinion is or is not reasonable is often a highly controversial determination; and the crucial question is what makes an opinion reasonable or unreasonable. It seems to me that the answer to this question is not encouraging for legal (and political) theory: the distinction between reasonable and unreasonable opinions may hinge on nothing more fundamental than whether an opinion is held among a certain elite. If one grows up in a society where 'pro-life' opinions are common among prominent or respected people, then one may properly conclude that this is a reasonable (if wrong) opinion. This may be all that there is to this reasonable/unreasonable business: the unrelated reasonableness of the people holding the opinion. Yet this distinction between reasonable and unreasonable opinions is of crucial importance: not only does it often influence our private actions, it is a distinction which marks decisive public lines in our increasingly pluralistic societies – and, as we shall see, it is a distinction upon which legal determinations are often based.

This important observation, and its implications for the difficulty of impartiality, will be discussed below. For now it is sufficient to realise that we expect all statutory requirements to have recognisable reasons, having to do with the features of their operative category, as to why they treat that category as they do; and that these reasons need be, well, reasonable. This means that a

---

11 Thus the problem with the checkerboard statutes examined so far was merely a special case of the kind of legal norms we find unacceptable: these were a good heuristic device, for they demonstrated a point by appealing to the extreme and unequivocal case; but the point is equally valid in cases that are less extreme – and more controversial.

strict-liability statute applying to cars but not to washing machines, if legislated, would be legislated on the premise that there is a reason having to do with the difference between cars and washing machines which explains this difference in treatment. Pointing to this fact may not provide us with an uncontroversial criterion for evaluating whether such a statute is or is not acceptable: we may very well disagree about the reasonableness of that reason. But it will begin to show us how we perceive and shape our laws and our legal practice.

Is all this significant?

Now it may be objected that all this is perfectly trivial: of course we expect our laws to be supported by reasonable reasons! But so what? We also expect them to be just, and intelligent, and efficient, and what have you; but all this is completely obvious and also completely uninteresting. There is nothing in these expectations to tell us anything insightful about the law.

This declaration misses much of what I said above: we do not merely expect statutes to be supported by reasonable reasons, we also expect these reasons to be publicly available, and to demonstrate a relation between the features of the operative category and the treatment to which a category is subjected. The attempt to analogise these expectations to the expectation that statutes be just or intelligent cannot work: we want *any* rule of conduct to be just or intelligent; but we want it to have a public reason related to the features of its operative category only when it appears in the form of a law. We do not think, for example, that the rules laid down by parents to their children ('never open this drawer'), or the rules army commanders lay down to their soldiers ('only those whose last names begin with the letters A to N get sniper training'), or the rules that religions lay down to their faithful ('you shall not shave your beard'), need have publicly available reasons having to do with their operative categories. We do, however, think this in the case of laws. The young Iranian who talks to VS Naipaul in *Beyond Belief* is expressing sentiments different from those of a religious devout, as he himself acknowledges, when he complains about a religious rule, saying: 'To me, the rules about beards have no logic. They don't say why. They just say "Do it".'[12]

In other words, we are not dealing with some general virtue (justice, intelligence, efficiency) with contingent links to our legal regulations: we are dealing with a principle that pertains specifically to our laws. Perfectly worthy regulations may be unacceptable as *legal* regulations because of this principle. This is what Dworkin's hypothesised checkerboard statutes show: there is nothing wrong with a rule imposing strict liability on cars but not on washing machines (people cautious about the impact of strict liability may reasonably conclude that this is a good option) – and yet this is an unacceptable statute. Here is another example: consider a regulation rewarding war veterans by

---

12 Naipaul, 1998, p 223.

granting them an exemption from parking regulations. There seems to be nothing immoral or unreasonable about this regulation (legislators and foreign diplomats have such an exemption). Yet any statute rewarding war veterans must do so in a way that is related to their status: if there is no relation between being a war veteran and an exemption from parking regulations, then such a regulation would be unacceptable as a statute.

Now a ruler who is unconstrained by the principles of a legal system may not care for such a demand: Saddam Hussein may nonchalantly have decided to reward his war veterans by allowing them to park anywhere they felt like parking. But our legislators operate differently: they legislate laws with public justifications having something to do with the features of their operative categories. So here is one insight we can derive from our principle of public reason: the process of designing laws is guided by principles which impose limitations on the *content* of our laws. The institution of a legal system places *substantive* limits on the exercise of power. The law's limitation on legislative power is not restricted to the frequently repeated idea that legislators are bound by their own laws: the law contains limitations that limit the regulative options themselves.

There are more practical insights to be gained here – insights about the proper standards of legal interpretation. Understanding that legislators craft laws with the principle of public reason in mind (whether consciously or not) has important implications to our understanding of statutes' *purposes* – itself often a decisive factor in their application. The section entitled 'Legislative intention' will deal with this issue. Furthermore, as we shall also see below, legal arguments and legal determinations also preserve this principle of public reason; and this means that understanding this principle may allow us to better comprehend what makes a convincing legal argument or a convincing legal determination. But before addressing all these important points, I would like to draw some parallels between what has been said so far and the work of Lon Fuller.

The knowability of the law

It is a matter of common understanding that one of the requirements of the rule of law is that the law be known. But the claims advanced in the preceding pages allow us to understand this requirement in a new light: the knowability we require of the law is not merely that its subjects be advised of the standards of conduct required of them (that the law be 'promulgated'), nor even that these standards be clear and intelligible; it is that they also know the *justification* for the treatment prescribed by the law. This gives a new meaning to the opposition between the rule of law and arbitrary government: this opposition runs deeper than the idea that arbitrary government does not work by way of publicly available standards. It is an opposition between standards of conduct that are *themselves* arbitrary and standards supported by recognised public justifications.

One legal scholar who touched on the idea of a public reason requirement was Lon Fuller. In his famous exploration of the 'inner morality' of the law, Fuller lists eight attributes we demand of our legal norms: we demand that they be general, promulgated, not retroactive, clear, non-contradictory, not requiring the impossible, that they be constant over time, and that there be a congruence between official action and declared rule.[13] This last requirement is described, in Fuller's little tale about a king who violates these requirements one after the other, as the lack of any 'discernible relation between [the king's judicial] judgments and the code they purported to apply'.[14] This depicts the requirement as one of congruence between legislative command and adjudicative execution; and it therefore obligates Fuller to get into a discussion about proper legal interpretation (that is, about what adjudicative execution is about). When he does, the idea of public reason is shown hidden in his very assumptions.

Fuller says that the 'best short answer' to the question of the principles of legal interpretation was given in 1584 by the Barons of the Exchequer when they met to consider the difficult case of one Heydon:

> It was resolved by them, that for the sure and true interpretation of all statutes in general (be they penal or beneficial, restrictive or enlarging of the common law) four things are to be discerned and considered:
>
> 1st What was the common law before the making of the Act.
>
> 2nd What was the mischief and defect for which the common law did not provide.[15]
>
> 3rd What remedy the Parliament hath resolved and appointed to cure the disease of the common wealth.
>
> 4th The true reason of the remedy; and then the office of all the judges is always to make such construction as shall suppress the mischief, and advance the remedy.[16]

Fuller then adds that 'the central truth of the Resolution in Heydon's case [is] that to understand a law you must understand "the disease of the common wealth" it was appointed to cure'.[17] He later comments: 'Some obscurity concerning the mischief sought to be remedied by a statute can be tolerated. But if this obscurity exceeds a certain crucial point, then no virtuosity in draftsmanship nor skill in interpretation can make a meaningful thing of a statute afflicted with it.'[18]

---

13 Fuller, 1969, pp 33–94. In fact, many of Fuller's requirements of the 'inner morality' of the law (as Fuller names them) *derive* from the requirement of public reason. I will return to this point.

14 Fuller, 1969, p 38.

15 Fuller adds that the word 'mischief' was used at the time in a sense meaning to describe 'a situation where things did not fit together, chunks of chaos not yet reduced through human effort to reasoned order'. Fuller, 1969, p 83 (fn 38).

16 3 Co Rep 7a, quoted in Fuller, 1969, p 89.

17 Fuller, 1969, p 83.

18 Fuller, 1969, p 83.

That 'mischief' is none other than the public reason of which we spoke. In elaborating on his idea Fuller makes use of an analogy where an inventor of household devices dies, leaving behind him an unfinished sketch of an invention. His son is bequeathed the task of completing that work. Fuller then argues that the son must discover what Fuller calls 'the intention of the design': the son 'would look to the diagram itself to see what purpose was to be served by the invention and what general principle or principles underlie the projected design'.[19] To explicate the analogy, the legal interpreter, looking at a statute, identifies the principles underlying its design and then uses these principles in determining what that statute requires. The reason underlying a law – the 'intention of its design' – must be in principle discernible from looking at it; and where it is not discernible, that statute is, as far as the law is concerned, hardly a 'meaningful thing'.[20]

II Legal interpretation

Once we note that all statutes possess publicly available reasons for their treatment of their operative category, it naturally follows that these reasons play a role in our interpretation of these statutes. (After all, don't we demand of statutes that they have public reasons for the very fact that their application vis-à-vis particular cases be publicly reasoned?) That role is easy to see in cases where the conditions stipulated for the operation of a statute are present, and yet the statute would be held inapplicable because its public reason fails in the case at hand. This happens, for example, when the features associated or correlated with a class, and for which the class is treated as the statute demands, are absent from an instance of that class. In Fuller's famous example, a monument consisting of a World War II truck is to be placed in a park where a legal rule prohibits the entry of vehicles.[21] Here the statute would not prohibit the entry of the truck because its public reason is simply inapplicable to the case. A similar though more difficult case was presented before the US Supreme Court in *Kaiser Aluminum & Chemical Corporation v Weber*, a case we encountered in Chapter 2.[22] The Court was called to decide whether a private corporation implementing an affirmative action policy where black employees received priority for training was in violation of Title VII of the Civil Rights Act which prohibits discrimination 'because of race'.[23] A white employee denied a place in the training program sued his employer, but the court held that these policies did not violate the statute. Underlying this decision was the determination that certain features *associated* with the

---

19 Fuller, 1969, p 86.

20 Fuller, 1969, p 83.

21 Fuller, 1958.

22 *Kaiser Aluminum & Chemical Corporation v Weber*, 443 US 193; 99 S Ct 2721 (1979).

23 Section 703(d), 78 Stat 256; 42 USC § 2000e-2(d).

practices prohibited by the statute, and for which these practices are prohibited, were lacking in the case at hand: the case, in other words, did not fit the statute's public reason.

The case of the ambulance entering the park on an emergency call presents another category of cases where the public reason of the statute obviously dictates its application: here the public reason *is* applicable (the case does present the problem the statute comes to address – the ambulance does pose a danger to pedestrians, it is noisy and polluting, and so on), but following the statute would come at an unreasonable price *given that public reason*. *United States v Kirby*, which we also previously met, was a similar case.[24] *Kirby* involved indictment brought against a sheriff for violation of an 1825 statute providing that 'if any person shall knowingly and wilfully obstruct or retard the passage of the mail ... he shall, upon conviction, for every such offence, pay a fine not exceeding one hundred dollars'.[25] A sheriff who arrested a man carrying US mail who was accused of murder was indicted under the statute. The US Supreme Court quashed the indictment, ruling that Congress had no intention to immunise postal workers from arrests and detention. It was unreasonable to apply the statute given that it meant to guarantee the quick delivery of US mail.[26]

---

24 74 US 482, 486 (1868).

25 74 US 482 (1868), quoting 4 Stat at Large 104.

26 A similar if more difficult example is the by now famous *Tennessee Valley Authority v Hill*, 437 US 153 (1978), where the US Supreme Court ordered the halt of a nearly completed hundred-million-dollar dam (whose construction began long before the rule's enactment) under the Endangered Species Act. The opening of the dam would have destroyed the only habitat of the 'snail darter', an obscure and uninteresting little fish. On its face, the statute called for halting the construction; but it was doubtful whether the preservation of a small and uninteresting species of fish justified pulling the plug on a project with substantial expected benefits, and one into which so much public money had already been poured. This is what made the case such a difficult one (with a reversal of the appeals court decision, and acrimonious exchanges between the majority and the dissenting opinions). As often happens, the real issue was hidden between peremptory declarations about the canons of statutory construction. The real bone of contention – whether the public reason of the statute pales into insignificance in the case – was certainly there, clearly visible when the opinion quoted a congressional committee report which said: 'it is in the best interests of mankind to minimise the losses of genetic variations. The reason is simple: they are potential resources. They are keys to puzzles which we cannot solve, and may provide answers to questions which we have not yet learned to ask. To take a homely, but apt, example: one of the critical chemicals in the regulation of ovulations in humans was found in a common plant. Once discovered, and analyzed, humans could duplicate it synthetically, but had it never existed – or had it been driven out of existence before we knew its potentialities – we would never have tried to synthesise it in the first place. Who knows, or can say, what potential cures for cancer or other scourges, present or future, may lie locked up in the structures of plants which may yet be undiscovered, much less analyzed? ... Sheer self-interest impels us to be cautious.' *Tennessee Valley Authority*, p 179. We shall see later what makes the ambulances on emergency calls an easy example and the snail darter a difficult one (the matter is not merely the strength or weakness of the interests involved).

These are all obvious instances of statutes' underlying public reasons figuring in the resolution of cases; but public reasons figure in the resolution of *all* cases, whether this is obvious or not: explicitly or implicitly, in the background or foreground, a statute's public reason is always a factor in its application. I am not saying – and it would be a mistake to say – that statutes' public reasons always determine their applicability: there are cases where a public reason fails and yet the statute applies.[27] But whether determinative or not, a statute's public reason is an essential factor in legal interpretation. Indeed the problem with checkerboard statutes, which have no identifiable public reason, is that they are not amenable to proper application. The application of checkerboard statutes can proceed only as the application of blind commands: legal reasoning stands helpless before them; it has nothing to grab on to, for it is precisely this link between the features of an operative category and the treatment it receives – so conspicuously missing here – that opens the way for the proper application of a statute.

Legislative intention

It should be clear by now that these public reasons have close affinity with what are famously known as the 'purposes' of statutes or their 'legislative intentions'. The use of 'legislative intention' in legal interpretation is the subject of some heated debates, both in academic circles and among practising legal professionals, and I would like to show how our new understandings bear upon these debates.

One illustrative approach to legislative intention as an interpretive tool can be found in Jeremy Waldron's *Law and Disagreement*, where the author pronounces:

> It is true that reference to legislative intent is reasonably common among judges and lawyers in America, and the appeal to 'original intent' is common too in the politics of American constitutional law. Philosophically, however, the idea of appealing beyond the statutory text to independent evidence of what particular legislators are thought to have intended has been subject to such powerful criticisms, most notably by Ronald Dworkin, that one is surprised to find it appearing again in anything other than a trivial form in respectable academic jurisprudence.[28]

These powerful criticisms often go as follows: it is meaningless – they say – to speak of a legislative intention where the legislature is a body made up of

---

27 Imagine that a statute designed to reduce petrol consumption grants tax exemptions for cars partially powered by electricity. An importer imports 1,000 such partly electrical cars which, however, perhaps unknown to the importer, happen to consume more gasoline than any comparable non-electrical vehicle. The government refuses to grant the expected tax exemption, and the importer takes her plight to the courts. Now although the public justification of the statute is inapplicable here, there may be good legal reasons to apply the statute anyway. In such cases the legal arguments for applying the statute must explain why the statute is to be applied despite the failure of its public reason.

28 Waldron, 1999, p 119 (footnotes omitted).

numerous individuals, each with her own ideas about the statute's intention (sometimes with no such ideas at all), and where the resulting legislative product may be the result of such political compromises as to conform to nobody's intention anyway.[29] Moreover, even if one could somehow overcome these difficulties, we would still face the following problem: legislative intention is an idea which can be formulated on radically different levels of abstraction, and the disposition of cases may simply depend on the level of abstraction at which one chooses to speak.[30] In short, legislative intention is an extremely speculative and manipulable idea that can offer no real guidance for legal interpreters.

These sweeping criticisms are to a large extent avoided once we understand legislative intention in terms of public reasons. To begin with, these criticisms attack a misconception of what legislative intention is really about: legislative intention is certainly not 'what particular legislators are thought to have intended' in passing a statute.[31] Discovering legislative intention is not an exercise in individual psychology: legislative intention is not a fact about what this or that legislator has thought. Rather, it is a hypothesis about the reason for which a certain category is treated in a certain way – and this reason is in principle always discoverable from the face of the statute (otherwise we would think that statute a checkerboard statute, and, generally speaking, there are no checkerboard statutes on our law books). It is what Lon Fuller called the 'the intention of the design': the intention of the statute expressed in its design and discoverable from consulting it.

Appeals to legislative intention, then, need not – and often do not – look 'beyond the statutory text to independent evidence of what particular legislators are thought to have intended'.[32] But even where such appeals are made – for example to legislative debates, to committee reports, to speeches given by the sponsors of a bill – they may be fully justified: legislative intention must be publicly available, but it need not be *obvious*; and such materials may be helpful, or indeed indispensable, in ascertaining it. (Imagine a statute prohibiting below-surface excavations in a certain area, or a statute prohibiting stores from opening on a certain date.) Such materials are certainly not *dispositive*, but they are often highly relevant: they often help legal practitioners formulate realistic hypotheses on a statute's *raison d'être*.[33]

'Legislative intention', correctly understood, also avoids the charge that it can be framed on widely different levels of abstraction, each recommending a

---

29 For some modern examples, see, eg, Dworkin, 1986, pp 313–27; Waldron, 1999, pp 119–46.

30 For a version of this criticism, see, eg, Linde, 1976, p 212.

31 Dworkin would certainly agree with my claim: Dworkin's criticism (and perhaps even Waldron's) is aimed not at what American judges and lawyers are talking about, but at what some of their (positivist) academic theoreticians are talking about.

32 Waldron, 1999, p 119.

33 A better hypothesis than the one suggested by such extra-textual materials may be formulated – whatever the legislators claimed, or actually believed, was the intention of the statute.

potentially different resolution to a case. Take the 'no vehicles in the park' example. The critic would like to say that this statute's legislative intention can range from the relatively specific intention to 'preserve park roads for walkers' to the highly abstract intention to 'create an agreeable place for park visitors'. These different legislative intentions may call for different resolutions of cases – indeed they seem to call for starkly different inquiries – so that appealing to legislative intention may allow legal interpreters to defend whatever claim they wish to support. But this charge is to a large extent avoided once we allow that the *correct* legislative intention relates the characteristics of an operative category (here 'vehicles') to the treatment demanded (the ban from the park). This means that the legislative intention of the 'no vehicles in the park' statute is neither the intention to preserve paths only for walkers, nor the intention to create a pleasant environment (although these two may very well be achieved by the statute): rather, it is the intention to keep the park free of certain *characteristics* associated with vehicles – their danger to pedestrians, their noise, or their pollution, for example. And whether a case does or does not fall under the statute's legislative intention depends, at least in part, on the degree to which the case poses these dangers.

Now this makes a big difference: according to the criticism, the way to hypothesise legislative intention is essentially to ask 'what does this statute seek to achieve?'. This question is, indeed, extremely open ended: many different things can be achieved by barring vehicles from parks. But the real question is quite different: the real question asks 'what features belonging to the category of vehicles explain barring them from the park?'. Here the options are much more limited. This does not mean, of course, that there are no options at all: there are, and people may disagree about which is the correct one. It may also remain unclear whether, and to what extent, the identified characteristics are present in the case. Appeals to legislative intention *can* be a ruse when justifying a resolution where intention, properly understood, cannot preclude a contrary conclusion. But these problems are to be distinguished from the sweeping criticism seeking to depict appeals to legislative intention as a front for discretion running wild: appeals to legislative intention are not as problematic, or as unconstrained or manipulable, as that criticism implies. In truth, as I said above, appeals to legislative intention are not even optional: whether made explicit or not, they are the heart of legal interpretation, for to know what a statute requires in a given case is to know, first and foremost, what is the reason for the treatment demanded by that statute, and how the case relates to that reason (even if, as I also said, legislative intention is not necessarily determinative as to the disposition of a case).

Racial segregation statutes in apartheid South Africa: public reason in action

An interesting illustration of the crucial role played by public reasons in the legislation and application of statutes can be glimpsed in an article by Arthur

Suzman, published in 1960 in South Africa, to which Lon Fuller refers in *The Morality of Law*.[34] The article documents the difficulties experienced by apartheid South African courts in settling on a definition of racial classifications. These classifications were, of course, of the utmost importance under apartheid: geographic place of residence and employment, education, the choice of a spouse, even tax rates – everything depended on one's classification under South Africa's categories of racial classification. Yet, despite the immense significance of this classification (or perhaps because of it), the South African legislature and the South African courts never ceased to waver between one classificatory criterion and another, creating a degree of uncertainty which resulted in a deluge of litigation. Suzman writes:

> Differential legislation based on race necessarily presupposed the classification and definition of the racial groups concerned. An examination of such legislation in the Union of South Africa reveals the absence of any uniform or consistent basis of race classification and presents a bewildering variety of statutory definitions of the various racial groups. The legislation abounds with anomalies and the same person may, in the result, fall into different racial categories under different statutes.[35]

The article proceeds to demonstrate not only a divergence of opinions across statutory schemes, but also habitual reversals and changes of course regarding the construal of one and the same piece of legislation.

Now what was the cause for all this? Why the endless wavering? The author of the article advances the following hypothesis:

> [T]he absence of uniformity of definition flows primarily from the absence of any uniform or scientific basis of race classification. Any attempt at race classification and therefore of race definition can at best be only an approximation, for no scientific system of race classification has as yet been devised by man. In the final analysis the legislature [and the courts] is attempting to define the undefinable.[36]

But this suggestion, though it goes in the right direction, only gives the beginning of an answer: after all, why can't legal classifications be based on categories with no scientific grounding whatsoever? Fuller's discussion of the problem is also rather brief. He says that: 'The simple demand that rules of law be expressed in intelligible terms seems on its face ethically neutral toward the substantive aims law may serve.'[37] But the problem with South Africa's segregation law shows us otherwise: 'Even the South African judge who in his private life shares the prejudices that have shaped the law he is bound to interpret and apply must, if he respects the ethos of his calling, feel a deep distaste for the arbitrary manipulations this legislation demands of him.'[38]

---

34 Fuller, 1969, p 160.
35 Suzman, 1960, p 339.
36 Suzman, 1960, p 367.
37 Fuller, 1969, p 159.
38 Fuller, 1969, p 160.

Let me precede my own take on the matter with the caveat that my explanation will not offer a full analysis of the problem either, but will only take us a few steps further than the short remarks made by Suzman and Fuller. The problem, to repeat, is essentially this: as regards to racial classifications cases, the South African courts made a mess of things; mutually irreconcilable decisions kept piling up, generating repetitive appeals and flooding the courts with racial classification cases. What caused this failure? The answer, as Fuller noted, pertains to what legal interpretation required of the South African courts. As we saw, one thing that the legal interpreter must do when applying a statute is ascertain the public reason of the relevant statute, and then ascertain how that public reason relates to the case at hand. In ascertaining the public reason of a statute the legal interpreter must establish those features of the relevant class which explain the treatment prescribed to it. It is in the light of this determination that the legal interpreter proceeds to ascertain whether, and to what extent, the features which explain the treatment are present or absent from the case. (Even if these features are absent, this need not mean that the case will be excluded from the prescribed class; but if it is not excluded, the court needs to explain why it is not.) In short, the decision as to whether a particular case falls within or without a legal category, and why it does – which is the exact decision the South African courts kept messing up – must be informed by the presence or absence of the features accounting for the treatment prescribed by the statute.

But here the South African courts faced a problem. The feature upon which racial segregation laws were based was the 'inferiority' or 'superiority' of the respective classes (some races were presumably superior to others, and were to remain superior by maintaining their 'purity'). But these features were of little help for the South African courts: not only were they incredibly vague and indefinite, and thus practically unascertainable; but their relation to the chosen legal categories of race was itself unsupportable. All this meant that the judges had to offer a definition of racial classifications which was independent of the very reason for which the statutes appealed to racial classifications to begin with. In other words, they had to turn to the free-floating notion of 'race'; but that notion, as Suzman said, could not offer them much guidance: there was simply no good (or 'scientific') method of racial classification.

In short, the South African courts were forced to draw lines in the sand: for instance, defining racial categories by reference to the birthplace of the parents, thereby deciding that a person must pay such and such taxes, or may not marry such and such a person, because her parents were born in Madagascar. But these definitions were as arbitrary as those they sought to refine: the relation between the features of the legal category and the treatment it received remained absent from the decision-making process. There was no surprise, then, that when the next case arrived and parental birthplace called for a racial classification which the courts found hard to swallow, they simply moved to draw a brand new line – referring to the social reputation of the person in question, for example. But a subsequent case would sooner or later face the court with another unacceptable result – and so on and so forth. The courts couldn't stick to their lines because, apart from a concern with administrative convenience, there was never a good reason to stick to them.[39]

III   The non-legal adjudicator and the judge

To summarise: I have been arguing that all statutes have publicly available reasons, having to do with the features of their operating categories, as to why these categories are treated as the statutes demand; that these public reasons must pass a threshold of reasonableness; that they are an important factor in establishing legal rights and duties; and that identifying those reasons is not as problematic a task as some proclaim. All this means that, perhaps in contradiction to the idea of legal interpretation prevailing in the popular mind, the difference between a judge sitting at law and a mere judicious adjudicator sitting in judgment does *not* consist in the fact that the judge follows authoritative rules which define in advance the conditions for their own applicability. Those conditions may be present where the rule is inapplicable – or absent where it applies. Still, legal interpretation is certainly unlike the decision-making of a mere judicious adjudicator. This seems obvious if only for the fact that judges operate, in one way or another, with a set of given rules. But the point is true even in the case of non-legal adjudicators who *also* operate with rules: legal interpretation imposes on the judge a set of constraints to which an adjudicator, striving to arrive at a just and intelligent resolution, may be utterly oblivious.

Imagine an adjudicator who is given a set of rules with which to work. Like the judge, the adjudicator must decide in each case whether there is a relevant rule, and then whether to apply that rule. (As with the judge, that decision does not turn exclusively on the conditions spelt out in the rule: the rule may be held inapplicable to cases where these conditions are present, or applicable to cases where they are not.) The adjudicator's *modus operandi* is therefore as follows: when a case arrives before her she consults her collection of rules to see whether there is any potentially applicable rule, and what that rule may require in the case. But she may refuse to follow the rule if what it requires appears to her grossly unjust or somehow unreasonable or absurd in its application to the given case – in which case she takes a fresh look at the case and at the reasons for resolving it one way or another. For instance, imagine a case where a party seeks to enforce a contract. A relevant rule holds the

---

39 All this suggests why an affirmative action statute may avoid such problems. Such statutes rely, to a large extent, on voluntary compliance with racial self-classifications, but if it came to defining racial categories, the courts might have something to grab on to when applying them. Affirmative action laws see a correlation between the category of race and past or present deprivation of opportunity caused by racist social perceptions. Whether the public reason of an affirmative action regulation applies to a certain person therefore depends on the extent to which that person was impacted by such past or present deprivations. This may not be a very fine definition, but it certainly avoids the arbitrary line-drawing which plagued the South African courts.

contract fully enforceable under certain conditions (knowledge of the facts, intention to be bound, and so on), all of which are satisfied in the case. Yet enforcing the contract would entail the loss of the lifetime savings of a person who entered into an unfavourable contract with a party far more cunning and experienced. Now the adjudicator may decide that it would be unreasonable to apply this rule to this case (the loss of lifetime savings, she thinks, is too high a price for such foolishness), and she may proceed to decide the case differently (perhaps some compensation will be paid). The rule having failed, the adjudicator resolves the case in the most judicious way she can find. Now the point I am making is that there are significant differences between the work of this adjudicator and the job of the legal judge – differences which constitute the true hallmark of the distinction between legal interpretation and non-legal adjudication.

One significant difference pertains to the very *sort* of considerations that each decision-making process may employ. Unlike the adjudicator's considerations, legal considerations need to be articulated, they need to be public, they need to be concrete, they must respect the public reason of an applicable legal rule, and they must manifest a link between the treatment for which they call and the class to which they apply. These constraints resemble, to some extent, Lon Fuller's famous list of eight attributes demanded of a law, and most of them derive from the public reason in which legal requirements need be grounded.[40] Let us examine them in detail.

Consistency

The law must settle on those considerations it deems dispositive: the law cannot allow cases which are identical in all relevant respects to be resolved differently using different considerations. Legal interpretation always looks upon a case as the representative of a class: a case stands for all the cases having identical representative features, and all these cases must be resolved in a similar manner. The requirement does not demand that legal considerations be fixed and frozen; only that whatever the legal considerations are, they would apply to all similar cases. Judges may change course; but such reversals must be done consciously, and with the acknowledgement that the reversal is applicable to all identical cases. The significance of this will become evident in the coming discussion on the requirement of articulateness. (I am ignoring here the issue of courts' hierarchy, where considerations handed down by a superior court are endowed with a status similar to that of legislation. On the relation between statutes and the considerations of legal interpretation, see below.) Note that this requirement of consistency must be distinguished from the idea of 'consistency over time' (as Fuller named his idea of consistency): the requirement is not that judges may not change course

---

40 As I said before, and as the following discussion shows, many of Fuller's attributes are derived from the demand that legal requirements be publicly justified. See Fuller, 1969, pp 33–38.

too often; the idea is that whatever course they have chosen must be understood as applicable to all cases having identical representative features, be them past, present, or future cases. If the judge cannot stomach this implication to his use of a legal consideration, then that consideration may not be used.

This, mind you, is not a constraint imposed on the non-legal adjudicator. The non-legal adjudicator need not 'settle' on any consideration: she may decide one case using certain considerations, and then an identical case using other ones, without considering for a moment whether this new resolution is similarly applicable to the previous case. Why would she decide these cases differently? Well, on different occasions she may feel differently about the matter (people do all the time); but unlike the judge, she is not obliged to make up her mind once and for all. Both decisions may seem to her equally judicious; and the fact that she need not consider the applicability of the considerations to the earlier case may allow differences which she herself would consider irrelevant to impact the difference in the solutions. Excellent adjudicators (or arbitrators) are not bound by the principle of consistency, and the range of considerations they can use is consequently much larger than the range available to legal interpreters.

Articulateness

Legal considerations (to the extent that they cannot be taken for granted or understood implicitly) must be *articulated*. The judge may feel that a certain disposition is proper, having a gut feeling about where the correct legal resolution lies; but where no articulated consideration can be adduced, those feelings must be ignored. This distinguishes the rule of law from the sort of adjudication made famous in Weber's discussion of '*Kadi* justice' – where the Muslim judge is supposed to *intuit* the resolution of the cases before him.[41] It also explains the celebrity status of certain judges, whose keen intelligence has improved the corpus of laws by pinpointing and articulating considerations which, until then, were legally irrelevant 'intuitions', forever prevented from properly impacting legal determinations.

The requirement of articulateness combines with the principle of consistency so as to impose certain important constraints on the work of judges. In 1999, when Spain requested the extradition of Augusto Pinochet from England for violations of human rights, the English Law Lords decided to bar any request for Pinochet's arrest and extradition for alleged crimes committed before 1988. Commenting on the grounds for this decision, an international lawyer derisively remarked that 'under this ruling, Hitler would have gotten away with it as well'. If true, that would mean that the Law Lords' decision is a bad decision at law. Now why is that? The reason derives from a combination of the requirements of articulateness and consistency. The

---

41 See Weber, 1978, pp 976–78.

problem with the Law Lords' decision is this: all international lawyers agree that were Hitler caught, no matter how late, he would have been extraditable for human rights violations under international law. This means that if Pinochet is to avoid extradition and trial, this must be for a reason which distinguishes his situation from Hitler's: after all, the two stand accused of essentially identical charges (despite Hitler's far more atrocious record) under essentially identical circumstances (as heads of state). This, as I noted above, is the principle of consistency: two identical cases must be resolved similarly. Sure enough, reasons for distinguishing Pinochet may exist: perhaps Pinochet's crimes were not of sufficient magnitude so as to override the doctrine of sovereign immunity, or perhaps Pinochet has many powerful supporters in Chile, and there is fear that Chile would be destabilised, or what have you. But if these are the considerations, then the judge must articulate them: the judge must come up with the principled reason for refusing the extradition so as to distinguish Pinochet's case from Hitler's, else we are facing either a violation of the principle of consistency, or a violation of the principle of articulateness: either way, we are facing a faulty decision.

Here is another example: in *Flagg Bros Inc v Brooks* the US Supreme Court rejected the claim that a warehouseman's sale of bailed goods to satisfy a lien – an action specifically authorised by New York's commercial laws – must pass constitutional scrutiny under the federal constitution.[42] Only acts of state or acts attributed to the state must pass constitutional scrutiny. But according to the court, the sale of the goods cannot be attributed to the state, although it was specifically authorised by state laws, because the state *permits* but does not *compel* the sale of the goods. So the sale of the goods was not an action that could violate the federal constitution because this action – although authorised by the state – was not compelled by it. The dissenters in the case took issue with this reasoning: under this rationale, they said, New York could pass an endless number of rather shocking laws which would never be subjected to constitutional scrutiny: for example, New York might authorise 'any person with sufficient physical power to acquire and sell the property of his weaker neighbour'; and this law – according to the considerations offered by the court – would not violate the constitution because it merely 'authorises' action but does not 'compel' it. But if we all agree that such a law would be in clear violation of the federal constitution (as presumably any lawyer would), then the considerations adduced by the court cannot justify the court's decision: there must be a further distinction between the above law and the law authorising the sale of the bailed goods that would justify treating them differently; and if the court cannot find any, then – as far as the law is concerned – the decision in the two cases must be the same.

Needless to say, the non-legal adjudicator is not bound by any requirement of articulateness. The non-legal adjudicator may decide cases according to her gut feeling, or according to considerations which are articulable but not

---

42 436 US 149 (1978).

articulated (perhaps there are good reasons for a decision which are best kept secret). Perhaps the best adjudicators are wise men and women with keen intuitions and pursed lips. But the judge's options are much more limited than the adjudicator's: the judge may not use a variety of considerations which the non-legal adjudicator, striving for a proper and just resolution, very well may.

Concreteness

The requirement of articulateness is further 'sharpened' by the requirement of concreteness. Legal considerations need not only be identified – their abstractness must also be checked. Overly vague considerations may not influence a legal decision. Here's an example: take a rule holding that 'a person shall be licensed to practise medicine if graduating from a recognised medical school and passing a qualifying exam'. A person secures a medical licence and opens a medical office. Soon thereafter the health authorities begin to receive numerous complaints of misdiagnoses. Eventually, the authorities seek to revoke the person's medical licence on grounds of incompetence, and the matter gets to the court. Now it may be obvious from the record that the person is indeed incompetent; and this may be perfectly sufficient for the non-legal adjudicator to have her licence revoked. But 'incompetence', standing alone, may not be sufficient grounds for the judge: the judge needs to give this term a clearer and more precise formulation if he wishes to use it as the ground for revoking a medical licence. He cannot simply say (as the adjudicator may): 'here we have a case of obvious incompetence, and, in the service of public health and in the service of justice, the licence is hereby revoked'. He needs to specify in what this incompetence consists: does it consist in the failure to administer the right treatment? And then what treatment was, or should have been, administered? Does the incompetence consist in the failure to diagnose certain disorders? And then why does the failure to diagnose these specific disorders constitute the grounds for the revocation? If no such specific considerations are brought to bear on the decision, no legal determination revoking the licence can be properly reached. The adjudicator may use any vague or unarticulated consideration she wishes to use; and both justice and public health may be well served by her decision. But the judge may safeguard justice and public health only by employing clear and specific considerations.

Here is another example: a statute requires the local authorities to allow demonstrations for groups wishing to express social, moral, or political beliefs. A group advocating certain extreme and offensive ideas wants to march in town, and the non-legal adjudicator swiftly concludes that the application of the rule to this obnoxious group is unwarranted, and that the demonstration should be prohibited. But, once more, the judge has a different problem on his hands: if he wishes to avoid the application of the rule he must ground that decision in a consideration that is clear – that is, a consideration that draws specific enough a distinction between the speech that this group wishes to express and the speech whose protection is warranted under the statute. The 'offensiveness' of the speech may be a sufficient consideration for the non-legal interpreter, but not for the judge: the judge must come up with a more specific reason, or else he must allow the speech to be treated as other speech is. Establishing legal rights and duties cannot become too obscure a matter, and the considerations feeding into legal determinations must go beyond a certain threshold of specificity and clarity.

Publicness

Legal considerations must be perceived as doing their job by the public at large, not merely by a small coterie. That 'the plaintiff is the daughter of Arthur Kosovitz' may be an important consideration for some people, including both parties to a dispute; but it may never be a *legal* consideration, since the public at large will not recognise in it a reason for anything. Thus many considerations that a person may deem both relevant and important are disqualified from weighing on the process of legal interpretation. The non-legal adjudicator is, of course, entirely free to use such considerations; and in many cases (for example, when the parties to the dispute all recognise the force of such a consideration) there will be nothing unjust or improper in her doing so. But *legal* interpretation, to repeat, cannot employ considerations whose force is not recognisable, in principle, by the subjects of the law as a whole.

The requirement of publicness is one among several legal requirements often confusingly bundled together under the title of 'generality'. The 'generality' required of the law has proved a rather elusive notion – a property whose justification and significance are far from clear. Perhaps the most common explanation for generality is the attempt to see in it a mere matter of bureaucratic efficiency – a requisite in the regulation of large classes of people and actions.[43] Fuller, who dismissed the 'efficiency' explanation as one more positivistic oversight, thought that the requirement of generality amounts to the demand that the law appear in the form of *rules*, and that generality therefore does not preclude laws from addressing proper names (as is sometimes claimed). He gave an example of a legal rule applicable to a proper name – 'a statute which establishes a tax collection office in Centerville' – which does appear perfectly proper; and he claimed that any requirement of generality going beyond the requirement of 'ruleness' belongs to the 'external morality' of law – it is not a requirement imposed by the nature of law but rather a matter of fairness which perfectly legal rules may or may not respect.[44]

---

43 See, eg, Hart, 1994, pp 20–21; see also Austin, 1879, pp 94–98. There have been many attempts to explain the requirement of generality: for a modern attempt, see, eg, Roberto Unger, who tries to link the idea of generality to the belief in natural law: 'Because natural laws are believed to apply to all countries and periods, the precepts they dictate must be addressed to very broadly defined categories of persons and acts. Therefore, generality in stating the rules of positive law and uniformity in applying them serve as a testimonial of fidelity to the higher law rather than as mere administrative convenience. No wonder that the effort to give content to the nebulous conceptions of generality and uniformity should become a major concern of political and legal thought.' Unger, 1976, p 80.

44 Fuller, 1969, p 47.

But although Fuller's example of a legal rule is perfectly acceptable, he was clearly in the wrong: the generality we require of our laws is not exhausted by the requirement that they appear in the form of rules; legal rules may certainly lack legally proper generality. One of the aspects of generality they may lack is *publicness* – itself a derivative of the requirement of public reason: we demand explanations as to why the state treats a certain category the way that it does, and these explanations must be accessible, in principle, to the public at large. That is why Fuller's own example is perfectly acceptable, while a statute decreeing that 'Roberto Zucko may exceed the speed limit by 20 mph' is not. There is, however, more to the issue of generality in the law, and I will return to that issue below.

Respect for the determination of a relevant statute

This is certainly one of the most difficult among the factors distinguishing legal from non-legal decision-making. *Legal* rules are no mere recommendations; they make determinations which the judge must always respect, even if he believes them misguided.[45] Still, the judge decides whether a legal rule is to be applied or not even in cases where the conditions stipulated in the rule are present. In what way, then, must legal rules always be respected (given that their requirements may be properly avoided)?

To understand what is meant by that requirement it is worth looking into Lon Fuller's exposition of the requirement of 'non-contradiction among authoritative rules' (which Fuller lists as one of the eight attributes of the rule of law). 'It is generally assumed', says Fuller, 'that the problem [of contradictions among laws] is simply one of logic. A contradiction is something that violates the law of identity by which A cannot be not-A'.[46] Things are in fact quite different:

> Let us take a situation in which a contradiction 'in the logical sense' seems most evident. In a single statute, we may suppose, are to be found two provisions: one requires the automobile owner to install new license plates on January first; the other makes it a crime to perform any labor on that date … We can certainly say on this procedure that it makes no sense, but in passing this judgment we are tacitly assuming the objective of giving a meaningful direction to human efforts. A man who is habitually punished for doing what he was ordered to do can hardly be expected to respond appropriately to orders given him in the future. If our treatment of him is part of an attempt to build up a system of rules for the governance of his conduct, then we shall fail in that attempt. On the other hand if our object is to cause him to have a nervous breakdown, we may succeed. But in neither event will we have trespassed against logic.[47]

In other words, evaluating contradiction among laws entails a reckoning with their purposes – with their public reasons. To assert that legal rules may not

---

45 Assuming their reasonableness.

46 Fuller, 1969, p 65.

47 Fuller, 1969, pp 65–66.

contradict each other is in essence to assert that they may not frustrate each other's purposes: legal rules must manifest respect for the determinations entailed by the public reasons of other rules.

The same is true concerning the relation between a legal rule and the considerations employed in applying it: legal considerations must show respect to the determination entailed by the public reason of a relevant legal rule. Let me give an example of what is meant by that. Take, once more, a 'no vehicles in the park' rule which mandates a heavy fine for those who violate it. The determination entailed by that rule's public reason is presumably that 'vehicles' danger, noise, and pollution warrant barring them from parks'. A man who drove through the park comes before a court. In deciding whether the rule is to be applied to his case the judge may not employ considerations which do not respect the determination above.

It is obvious that the judge may not exonerate the man on the grounds that vehicles' danger, noise, and pollution do not justify barring them from the park (that would be an outright contradiction of the relevant determination); but respect for the rule's determination also applies to considerations that do not amount to outright contradictions. For instance, suppose the man is exonerated on the grounds that he drove through the park very slowly with his lights flashing; or on the grounds that his daughter was late for school and he was taking a short cut. These considerations do not directly contradict the rule, and yet they are, arguably, improper reasons for such legal resolutions: they essentially repudiate the rule's determination that vehicles' danger, noise and pollution warrant their exclusion from parks. Yet if the man is exonerated because he drove through the park in an effort to escape a murderer then, arguably, no disrespect for the rule is present. Unlike the former considerations, the latter does not appear to repudiate the public reasons underlying the adoption of the rule;[48] it still respects the determination that vehicles' danger, noise and pollution constitute a nuisance which warrants their exclusion from parks.[49]

What consideration 'respects' the rule and what doesn't is often a controversial question; but it is a question that judges must ask themselves regarding the considerations they employ. Legal interpreters know that while rules may prove inapplicable, the determinations they represent may not be repudiated: the legislature (or a judicial authority) has chosen a certain course of action from among the available alternatives, and the legal interpreter is bound to respect that choice even while recognising that the choice has its limits – that there are cases in which the assumptions underlying the adoption

---

48 Dworkin's analogy of a chain novel is most appropriate here: the legal interpreter operates from within a system of rules which she is obliged to respect; every legal decision must constitute an extension or a continuation of that system, not a break with it. See Dworkin, 1986, p 232.

49 See Raban, 2000, for a criticism of judicial decisions which failed to respect the determination of a relevant legal rule (more precisely, of a relevant constitutional doctrine).

of the rule do not hold, or where these assumptions do hold but the circumstances of the case make the rule an unreasonable choice of action. Our adjudicator, once more, is not restricted in this manner: when a case comes before her and she decides not to apply a rule, it may very well be for considerations which show little respect for the determination represented by the rule and its public reasons. By hypothesis, the adjudicator's rules do not enjoy the same status that legal rules do. Her rules can resemble the rules governing academic committees: there is always a point where these rules will be put aside for reasons contradicting the rationale for their very adoption. If we move to endow these rules with the same status they enjoy for legal interpreters, we have also moved a system of non-legal regulation closer towards a system of law.

Explaining the dispensed treatment

Finally, the features of the categories to which legal considerations apply must explain the specific treatment for which these considerations call. This is the principle of public reason as it plays itself in legal interpretation. The principle may sound like a truism; for to say that there is a consideration for treating X in a certain way seems to imply that there is something in X that explains that treatment. But a consideration may lack the *specificity* that the legal discourse requires. Take a case where the government files a claim against a decorated war veteran for adding a room to his house without the appropriate license. An adjudicator may consider it just and proper to exempt the distinguished veteran from the operation of the relevant statute, but the veteran status of the defendant cannot be a consideration for exemption for a judge: there simply seems to be no explanation as to why a decorated war veteran need not secure a license for improving his property. The legislature may not legislate checkerboard statutes, and neither may the judge. After all, legal interpretation, like legislation, is in the business of formulating legal rules: the disposition of any legal case must itself assume the form of a valid legal rule.

The crucial difference between the judge and the non-legal adjudicator does not consist in the fact that the judge follows pre-determined rules, but in the sort of considerations he can use. The judge may only use considerations of a certain *form*, whereas the non-legal adjudicator may use many other considerations while showing both cleverness and regard for justice. Legal considerations need to be consistent, articulated, concrete, and public; they must respect the public reason of a relevant legal rule, and they must explain the specific treatment for which they call. This is the case whether the decision can or cannot function as precedent: the concern here is not with future applications, but with publicly explaining the disposition of a case. These requirements no doubt limit a legal decision's potential for partiality when compared to non-legal decision-making: the legal interpreter, in other words, has much less 'discretion'. Nevertheless, these requirements do not eliminate the possible use of *preferences* in legal decision-making. Sure enough, many preferences are often excluded due to these requirements; but under certain circumstances, preferences do qualify as perfectly legal considerations. Partiality, broadly understood as we defined it above, is sometimes an inevitable feature of legitimate and valid legal determinations. This is the inevitable price of our commitment to the rationality of legal interpretation.

Chapter 7
Law and impartiality: conclusion

Let us remind ourselves of legal theory's concern over partial legal interpretation: it involves the use of preferences – controversial beliefs which do not appear to be true or false, so that the choice among conflicting alternatives appears unjustifiable as a matter of principle. We also said that this choice often appears to reflect the self-interest of the chooser; that the use of such beliefs as considerations in legal determinations can consistently benefit or injure certain individuals or groups; and that these considerations include a host of political, moral, and social beliefs whose relevance to many legal questions is beyond dispute. Thus, it is at least conceivable that such preferences play an inescapable part in legal interpretation – in which case impartial adjudication is an unattainable ideal. (We also said that the problem with preferences remains even if one admits, *arguendo*, that many of them *can* be characterised as true or false, as long as one concedes – as indeed one must – that these 'truths' are the subject of pervasive disagreements among reasonable and well informed people.)

As we saw, the understanding of law presented in the previous chapter does not rule out the use of preferences in proper legal interpretation: on the contrary, it argues that, under certain common circumstances, the duties of legal interpretation compel the legal interpreter to appeal to her preferences. Naturally, there are many considerations of preference which are excluded from proper legal decision-making (for instance, all those preferences which lack concreteness or publicness, or those which fail to justify the specific treatment for which they call); but often a legal interpreter will legitimately employ a consideration of preference while engaged in a perfectly valid legal determination. Valid legal determinations are sometimes partial. We must draw a distinction between wrong determinations and determinations which are legally correct but which could have come out otherwise. To be sure, this is no news for most legal theorists (and certainly not for legal practitioners); but different legal theories have radically different accounts of how preferences come into play in legal determinations, and different understandings about the pervasiveness of this phenomenon.

What is at stake in these different accounts? The principal significance of such theories is that they allow us to better evaluate the validity of legal claims and determinations, and they help us to better shape the structure of our legal institutions. Lawyers or judges need not be acquainted with legal theories in order to perform to the highest professional standards – just as a musician need not be acquainted with music theory in order to be a brilliant musician, a language speaker need know nothing about grammatical theory in order to speak perfectly, and an artist can produce works of genius without being acquainted with art theory. All these people possess some sort of understanding about the nature of their practice, but that understanding may be neither articulated nor explicit. Yet, explicit, articulated theories may have important things to tell musicians, language speakers, artists, and lawyers.

While some may perfectly master the principles of proper practice intuitively (like the musician who intuitively grasps the correct principles of composition), others may need explicit guidance in order to perfect their performance. Legal interpretation is a unique activity with its own set of rules and constraints, and if you get these constraints wrong (for instance, if you wrongly inflate the weight to be given to the conventional meanings of legal classificatory terms, or if you think that reliance on legislative records would be a violation of proper legal interpretation) then your legal argumentation or legal decision-making will suffer. Legal theory can help guide lawyers and judges towards a better appreciation of the correct principles of their work. Legal theory may also have much to say to those who already master those principles, by way of improving their self-understanding: legal theory may articulate principles with which they already operate but of which they may be utterly unaware, thereby giving them an analytical tool with which to evaluate legal arguments, or the worthiness of their working principles. Conquering the unconscious is a path to progress.

Finally, legal theory may have much to say about our institutional structures. There can be no doubt that the possible partiality of proper legal interpretation, for example, has an impact on our best institutional arrangements. For instance, that possibility raises the danger that valid legal determinations would consistently privilege one set of the legally valid alternatives so as to accord with the interests of a particular group: the legal system may become a vehicle for the advancement of interests in a way that is not intended by the legislature, and that may lend the advancement of these interests a legitimacy and permanence they would not have enjoyed otherwise.[1] One institutional response to this danger is a diverse judiciary – a feature which may be far less important under a system having one correct set of legal answers, or under the methodology of legal interpretation described by HLA Hart's legal positivism.

Much that is practical and important is at stake in our theoretical account of judicial impartiality and its relation to proper legal interpretation.

---

1   This point underlies some of the famous critiques of legal practice. According to Duncan Kennedy, for example, judicial decision-making is 'the vehicle of ideological projects': judges often make legal claims and legal determinations that are influenced by their ideological beliefs. Kennedy, 1997, p 1. According to Kennedy, *ideology* is a set of preferences: Kennedy says that there is no right ideology or wrong ideology (at least not so far as we can tell), that it is controversial, and that it is deeply related to the *interests* of the group of people adhering to it. See Kennedy, 1997, p 291.

A final word

Morton Horwitz has remarked that he fails to detect in the law the 'unqualified human good' some people see in it: the law, says Horwitz, creates 'formal equality' – 'a not inconsiderable virtue', he says – but it may also perpetrate and perpetuate substantive injustice 'by creating a consciousness that radically separates law from politics, means from ends, processes from outcomes'.[2] I disagree. The consciousness of the legal decision-making process is *not* concerned with mere formal equality, but with substantive equality through and through: it is grounded in a means/ends analysis, in justification and debate, and in reason – even if it often reaches conclusions with which we disagree. Still, by insisting that each and every legal requirement be grounded in reason and justified according to public standards, the law *is* an 'unqualified human good' – the goodness that is entailed by rejecting the arbitrary.

2   Horwitz, 1977, p 566.

Bibliography

Austin, J, *Lectures on Jurisprudence*, 4th edn, 1879, London: John Murray

Benjamin, M, *Splitting the Difference: Compromise and Integrity in Ethics and Politics*, 1990, London: University Press of Kansas

Berlin, I, *The Crooked Timber of Humanity*, 1990, London: John Murray

Campbell, T, *The Legal Theory of Ethical Positivism*, 1996, Aldershot: Dartmouth

Cohen, F, 'Transcendental Nonsense and the Functional Approach' (1935) 35 Col LR 809

Cohen, M (ed), *Ronald Dworkin and Contemporary Jurisprudence*, 1984, London: Duckworth

Coleman, J, 'Negative and Positive Positivism' (1982) 11 Journal of Legal Studies 139

Dworkin, RM, 'Hart's Postscript', paper presented at Oxford University HLA Hart Lecture Series, 2000

Dworkin, RM, 'Objectivity and Truth: You'd Better Believe It' (1996) 25 Philosophy & Public affairs 87

Dworkin, RM, *Law's Empire*, 1986, London: Fontana

Dworkin, RM, *A Matter of Principle*, 1985, Cambridge, Mass: Harvard UP

Dworkin, RM, 'Ronald Dworkin: Response', in Cohen, M (ed), *Ronald Dworkin and Contemporary Jurisprudence*, 1984, London: Duckworth

Dworkin, RM, *Taking Rights Seriously*, 1977, Cambridge, Mass: Harvard UP

Dworkin, RM, 'The Model of Rules' (1967) 35 University of Chicago LR 14

Endicott, T, 'Herbert Hart and the Semantic Sting' (1998) 4 Legal Theory 283

Fish, S, 'Wrong Again' (1983) 62 Texas LR 299

Fish, S, 'Working on the Chain Gang: Interpretation in Law and Literature' (1982) 60 Texas LR 551

Fiss, O, 'Objectivity and Interpretation' (1982) 34 Stanford LR 739

Ford, RT, 'The Boundaries of Race: Political Geography in Legal Analysis' (1994) 107 Harvard LR 1841

Foucault, M, *The History of Sexuality*, Hurley, R (trans), 1979, London: Allen Land

Frankfurter, F, 'Some Reflections on the Reading of Statutes' (1947) 47 Col LR 527

Freud, S, *Introductory Lectures on Psychoanalysis*, Strachey, J (trans), 2nd edn, 1966, New York: WW Norton

Freud, S, *Totem and Taboo*, Brill, AA (trans), 1960, New York: Vintage

Fuller, L, *The Morality of Law*, 2nd edn, 1969, New Haven: Yale UP

Fuller, L, 'Positivism and Fidelity to Law – A Reply to Professor Hart' (1958) 71 Harvard LR 630

Gallie, WB, 'Essentially Contested Concepts' (1956) 56 Proceeding of the Aristotelian Society 167

Gardner, J, 'Legal Positivism: 5½ Myths' (2001) 46 AJJ 199

Gordon, RW, 'Unfreezing Legal Reality: Critical Approach to Law' (1987) 15 Florida University LR 195

Habermas, J, *Between Facts and Norms*, Rehg, W (trans), 1996, Cambridge: Polity

Hart, HLA, *The Concept of Law*, 2nd edn, 1994, Oxford: Clarendon

Hart, HLA, 'Positivism and the Separation of Law and Morals' (1958) 71 Harvard LR 593

Hart, HM and Sacks, AM, *The Legal Process: Basic Problems in the Making and Application of Law*, 2001, New York: Foundation Press

Horwitz, MJ, 'The Rule of Law: An Unqualified Human Good?' (1977) 86 Yale LJ 561

Kennedy, D, *A Critique of Adjudication*, 1997, Cambridge, Mass: Harvard UP

Kennedy, D, 'Form and Substance in Private Law Adjudication' (1976) 89 Harvard LR 1685

Kramer, M, 'Dogmas and Distortions: Legal Positivism Defended' (2001) 21 OJLS 673

Kramer, M, *In Defense of Legal Positivism: Law Without Trimmings*, 1999, Oxford: OUP

Kress, K, 'Legal Indeterminacy' (1989) 77 California LR 283

Kronman, AT, *Max Weber*, 1983, Palo Alto: Stanford UP

Leiter, B, 'Rethinking Legal Realism: Toward a Naturalized Jurisprudence' (1997) 76 Texas LR 267

Lévi-Strauss, C, *Structural Anthropology*, Jacobson, C and Schoepf, BG (trans), 1968, London: Penguin

Linde, HA, 'Due Process of Lawmaking' (1976) 55 Nebraska LR 197

MacCormick, N, 'A Moralistic Case for A-moralistic Law' (1985) 1 Valparaiso LR 20

Mackie, J, 'The Third Theory of Law', in Cohen, M (ed), *Ronald Dworkin and Contemporary Jurisprudence*, 1984, London: Duckworth

Naipaul, VS, *Beyond Belief*, 1998, New York: Random House

Pareto, V, *The Mind and Society*, Bongiorno, A and Livingston, A (trans), 1935, London: Cape

Raban, O, 'Content-Based, Secondary Effects, and Expressive Conduct' (2000) 30 Seton Hall LR 501

Rawls, J, *A Theory of Justice*, 1971, Cambridge, Mass: Harvard UP

Raz, J, 'Two Views of the Nature of the Theory of Law' (1998) 4 Legal Theory 249

Raz, J, 'The Relevancy of Coherence' (1992) 72 Boston University LR 273

Raz, J, 'Dworkin: A New Link in the Chain' (1986) 74 California LR 1103

Raz, J, 'Legal Principles and the Limits of Law' (1972) 81 Yale LJ 823

Singer, J, 'Legal Realism Now' (1988) 76 California LR 465

Stavropoulos, N, 'Hart's Semantics', in Coleman, J (ed), *Hart's Postscript*, 2001, Oxford: OUP

Stavropoulos, N, *Objectivity in Law*, 1996, Oxford: OUP

Suzman, A, 'Race Classification and Definition in the Legislation of the Union of South Africa 1910–1960' (1960) Acta Juridica 339

Trubek, DM, 'Max Weber on Law and the Rise of Capitalism' (1972) 72 Wisconsin LR 720

Unger, RM, *Law in Modern Society*, 1976, New York: Free Press

Waldron, J, 'Normative (or Ethical) Positivism', in Coleman, J (ed), *Hart's Postscript*, 2001, Oxford: OUP

Waldron, J, *Law and Disagreement*, 1999, Oxford: Clarendon

Weber, M, *Economy and Society*, Roth, G and Wittich, C (eds), Fischoff, E (trans), 1978, Berkeley: University of California Press

Winch, P, *The Idea of a Social Science*, 2nd edn, 1990, London: Routledge

Index